How NOT to Buy a Cruising Boat

T.J. and Deb Akey

DEDICATION

We dedicate this book to you, our family, friends, and loyal blog readers who have made this journey possible through your knowledge, patience and support.

CONTENTS

The photograph of Kintala in the inset on the cover is the property of John Dakins, who graciously allowed us to use it to consruct the cover. It is by far the most perfect picture of Kintala we have under sail.

ACKNOWLEDGMENTS, DISCLAIMERS, AND INTRODUCTION

We are infinitely grateful to all those who have generously shared their experience with us over the past seven years. People taught us to sail, put up with our fumbling incompetence, listened to our endless observations and patiently answered our questions. Boulder Yacht Club and Tradewind Yacht Club members: you know who you are.

Several blogging cruisers answered our questions via email and blog post comments even though they had never even met us. They began as mentors and have become life-long friends. At the risk of missing someone, I'm not mentioning names but you know who you are as well.

A special thanks goes to our investment guru, Craig, and his office manager Linda, who never wavered in their belief that we could pull it off. Without their help we would not be here.

No books, blogs, marinas, sailing schools or instructors were paid or otherwise compensated for their mention in this book. We mention them only because they have been a positive influence and you may benefit from them as well.

All trademarked products contained within this publication are referenced as nominative fair use in critical review without the owners' permission. Under no circumstances is there any ownership or sponsorship stated or implied by the authors.

Much of this book is pulled from the knowledge recorded in seven years of blog posts on www.theretirementproject.blogspot.com. It's geared mostly to those dreaming of a life of cruising that have little or no previous sailing or boat-buying experience and are unsure of how to proceed. We made many mistakes along the way and, as a result, had a more difficult time getting started. This is the book we wish we had read before beginning our journey. Our hope is that by reading this book you will be spared the mistakes that we made and have a happy, successful cruising experience. Making a decision to go cruising is a highly personal one, and your experience may differ. *We make no claim to knowing the right way to do it, as there is no right way. There is only the right way for you.*

1 SO YOU WANNA BE A CRUISER

It was a dark and stormy night. Really, it was. I was working on the computer upstairs in our condo in the eclectic part of St. Louis, MO known as the Central West End, massaging my Quicken files and wondering if there was any possible way that two people firmly entrenched in a lifetime of aviation could possibly afford to retire. Ever. Don't even think *early*.

We've always loved the water, choosing our vacation spots along the ocean if possible, and if not, then near rivers or lakes. Our vacations were usually camping or on motorcycles, so budget living in small spaces was a no-brainer. A houseboat came to mind, only because they have room on their rear decks for motorcycles, and we were at that time doing a lot of long-distance riding on our bikes. A houseboat could be kept on one of the many rivers in St. Louis, allowing excursions to explore but also an affordable waterfront home near the kids when stationary. Then daughter #2 moved to Cape Cod. Uh-oh. No rivers went all the way from St. Louis to Cape Cod.

Maybe we needed to look at a cruising motor yacht so we could go down the Mississippi, around Florida, and up the East Coast. Some affordable ones were out there, so no problem until you begin to do the fuel math. We had a motor yacht owner once brag to us that his yacht was fantastic on fuel. It traveled 9 knots and did it on 3 gallons per hour. Hmmm...3 miles to the gallon...3000 miles...1000 gallons...$6,000 in 2007 dollars. Yeah...without side trips. OK, so no cruising motor yacht. Sailboat?

Google, being its intrusive and scary-smart self, determined by my search of "sail from St. Louis to Cape Cod" that I wanted sailing lessons in St. Louis (even before *I* knew I wanted sailing lessons in St. Louis), and popped up a sidebar ad for St. Louis Sailing Center. Who knew? I could not imagine any place in or near St. Louis that one could take sailing lessons, and we'd lived there 13 years by this point. I was quite surprised to say the least, but it was Friday night, though, so a call would have to wait till the morning.

Our condo has a landing half way down the stairs with some openings in it that look through to the living room below. I leaned my elbows into the opening and said to my ever-unsuspecting husband reclining in his comfy chair below, "What would you think about retiring onto a boat?" I wish I had had the forethought to hide a camera somewhere to record the

1

expression on his face. It was priceless. "Um...OK?" Deer in the headlights. Definitely deer in the headlights.

You might be wondering by now why this book about buying a boat starts with this chapter. It's impossible to discuss buying a cruising boat without first understanding the basis of what it means to be a cruiser and how you arrived at wanting that for yourself. It requires a level of personal honesty that, quite frankly, not many people are willing to possess. Being honest with yourself might mean realizing that your dream is not viable for you. Very few are able to acknowledge that fact and choose instead to live in denial, setting themselves up for failure right from the start. Ready for some tough stuff? We'll look at the following questions in the rest of this chapter:

- Why do you want to be a cruiser?
- What kind of cruiser do you think you are?
- How capable are you of doing the work?
- How willing is your significant other?
- What are your expectations?
- Can your cruising kitty support your expectations?

Why do you want to be a cruiser?

It's interesting to sit around at the cocktail hour cruisers call "sundowners" listening to the stories of how other cruisers got started. Cruisers come in all shapes, sizes, ages, colors and socioeconomic backgrounds. Their reasons for cruising are just as varied. Some are disenchanted with the status quo in our society and are choosing to distance themselves. Others are wanderers at heart and love exploring new places and cultures. Some choose it because it's an economically sensible way to live in a not so economically sensible society. Still others are cruising because it means living with the smallest possible footprint on the environment. Dangers lurk when your choice to go cruising is based on escape from your problems: a relationship gone bad, a recently lost loved one, depression, mountainous debt. A big misconception that bites potential cruisers is that going cruising will remove you from the consequences of your problems. The reality is that your problems will follow you, because your problems are not external to you, your problems are *within* you. If you are prone to depression on land, the hard parts about cruising will get you down. If you're prone to over-spending on land, you'll do the same while cruising. If you have a drinking problem on land it will only get much worse while cruising. Deal with the problems before you go, then reward yourself with cruising.

What kind of cruiser do you think you are?

When potential cruisers think about cruising, the picture that comes to mind is a white, sandy beach with a hammock swaying between palm trees where you are lying with a cold drink and a book, looking out at your perfect sailboat swinging into the wind in crystal-clear, aquamarine waters. It is sometimes like that, as

West End Bahamas

evidenced by this picture. I took it in the Bahamas at Old Bahama Bay Resort in the West End, a common place for cruisers to check in to the Bahamas. Especially in the early stages of cruising, where experience and knowledge are still being developed, I can tell you that this picture and the accompanying experience can be quite rare unless you have more money than God. So, if that isn't everyone's experience of cruising, then what is? It depends. It depends on what kind of cruiser you initially think you want to be, then how you deal with the kind of cruiser you discover you really are after an honest evaluation.

One of the really smart things we did in the six years of planning for this lifestyle was to take three trips in 2010. We took a trip with a sailing school from Tom's River in NJ to Block Island, around the island and west through Long Island Sound, down through the city of New York to Sandy Point, then back around the point and south to return to Tom's River in 7 days. We chose the school because it used a Pearson 35, the smallest boat we thought we could live on full time without killing each other. The next class was our ASA-114 catamaran course on a Lavezzi 40 in Pensacola Beach. We were still in the whole monohull vs. catamaran debate at the time so we chose this course to evaluate the catamaran. The final trip was John Kretschmer's Bahamas Bash, a 6-day trip on his beloved Kaufman 47 *Quetzal* from Ft. Lauderdale to West End, Bahamas, south around the Berry Islands, and back via Bimini. We took this trip because we believed the 47 to be the biggest boat we could handle safely with just the two of us. So what did we learn?

We learned that 35 feet is too small for us. It's a great size for a lot of people as evidenced by the fact that there are a lot of people out there cruising on boats even smaller. It's just too small for *us*. If we had a checkbook that wouldn't have bounced merrily out of the bank, we would have written a check for the Lavezzi the second day of class and called home to tell the kids to sell everything, including the house. We loved the boat and would have been very happy on a catamaran. The reality of our finances made a catamaran an unrealized dream. It was fitting that the training voyage with John Kretschmer was the last one. The old saying "the third time's the charm" was certainly true for us. While we realized 47 feet was a bit too much boat for just the two of us, we loved the style of *Quetzal*, the way she handled, her interior looks and her cutter rig.

Those three trips were our first and only foray into true blue water sailing. All of our previous sailing experience had been on our small, shallow Lake Carlyle in Illinois. We were enthralled. We loved the cruising lifestyle, we loved the sailing, we loved the wide expanses of ocean with no one else to be seen in any direction. It led us to believe that we were blue water sailors, and we began the search for a hard core blue water boat.

After more than a year of cruising, we've discovered that open ocean crossings are one thing when you're in someone else's boat with a crew of six. The same ocean crossings are quite another thing when your risk exposure includes everything you own, and you only have a crew of two, one of whom is likely to be sick, tired, or injured at any given time. With a larger crew, there is always someone else to help with sail changes or meal preparation. With a crew of two, you have to make it happen, no matter how you feel. You are, for the most part, single-handing in two separate shifts. While things may change with the accumulation of experience, it appears we're more coastal cruisers than blue water sailors. Had we the benefit of a book like the one you're holding, we might have chosen a different boat. I tell you this story because, even being honest with yourself and doing everything you can to try to determine what kind of cruiser you're likely to be, you can only make decisions with the information you have available; you need to be flexible and willing to change. I never really thought much about it at all until a good friend of ours came to visit us for two weeks in the islands. He wanted to try actual cruising in a cruising boat and when we gave him the chance to sum up what his impressions were at the end of the two weeks, he decided he was more of a live-aboard than a cruiser. A good lesson learned without the budget-busting investment of buying a blue water boat. There are several cruisers out there with Coast Guard licenses that are offering one or two week trips on their cruising sailboats so that you can have the opportunity of seeing it firsthand without any sugar coating. If you can locate one of these, I suspect it would go a long way toward giving you an honest view of what cruising is really like.

In deciding what kind of cruiser you think you might become, consider the common styles of cruising: commuter cruising, marina dwelling, mooring field living, and anchoring. I'll also add living aboard, although by its very static nature it can't really be included in cruising.

Commuter cruising is part-time cruising: living on land part of the year and on a boat part of the year. A lot of Canadian residents do this because I'm told that they have to live in country five months per year or they lose their government funded health care. Another reason for doing this is family. The time on land gives you ample time to get your grandbaby fix, and the cruising time makes you miss them again. It means having a pretty healthy bank account or some sort of telecommuting job you can do from the boat, since keeping both land residence and boat residence at the same time can be quite expensive.

Marina dwelling is also a form of commuter cruising where you cruise intermittently and spend long stretches of time on the dock. The advantages of dock living are many: hot showers, laundry, restaurants, air conditioning, endless power and water, easy access to pump-out, and more social interaction. The disadvantages are also many: noise, lack of ventilation, too many rules, very little privacy and often a restricted view. The biggest disadvantage, though, is the cost. Our slip in Cooley's Landing in Ft. Lauderdale went from an already high $805 per month off season to $1,689 per month in season. Those are 2014 three-month rates, already discounted from the monthly rate. If you're planning on the amenities of a marina to augment your cruising, cost is definitely a consideration. Even if you're not *planning* on many marina stays, they will sneak up on you—it's late and you can't reach the anchorage, somebody's too sick to anchor, you're picking up someone from the airport, it's too cold to anchor without heat, you need fuel or water or pump-out—the lure is tremendous. Cost for a 42-foot boat for transient nights can run from under a dollar a foot per night in Bimini to $8.50 per foot per night in some resorts in Florida. If you're on any kind of restricted budget and need to use a marina occasionally, planning is the key. Use a resource like ActiveCaptain.com to scope out marinas and to have pricing information and cruiser reviews prior to your stay.

Living on a mooring ball is good middle ground for a lot of cruisers. The cost is dramatically cheaper, the ventilation and the view are greatly improved, and most of the amenities are usually available via dinghy or water taxi, depending on the mooring field. As an example, Dinner Key in Coconut Grove—south of Miami, FL—has all the amenities of a marina including laundry, showers, a good dinghy dock, a water taxi, close restaurants, groceries, and chandleries at a rate of $20 a night or $300 a month (2015). The skyline view of Miami is the best to be found but it comes with a cost. The mooring field is very exposed and the water can be rough a good bit of the time. The balls in the mooring field are some of the most well-maintained we've encountered, though, so we would trust them through all but the worst of storms. The mooring field at Vero Beach is much more protected, has all the same amenities, but it also comes with a cost: prolific bugs most of the year and rafting to another boat on the same mooring ball is mandatory if they are crowded. It doesn't bother us, but it bothers some.

Anchoring is clearly a preferred option for those of us who are budget-driven. The reduced cost of anchoring allows you to stretch your cruising budget by as much as five or six times. One of the advantages of anchoring over any other means of cruising is the peaceful nature of most anchorages. I say *most* because some anchorages close to city limits are fraught with weekend boater antics that can try your patience. There's a certain freedom in picking a beautiful spot in a small cove somewhere and dropping the hook. It's more secluded, so if socializing is your deal then you have to make a concerted effort at dinghying over to other boats to introduce yourselves. Anchoring can also be more satisfying as it demands more skill and attentiveness to your surroundings and weather so that you don't drag into other boats or the shore. Sitting in your cockpit eating dinner as the sun sets, feeling pretty good about the day's travel, and realizing that you're not glued to the news with all its impending doom, all bring a sense of accomplishment and deep satisfaction that very few other means of living provide.

That is, after all, what cruising is about: an alternate form of living, which is the reason I'll include living aboard here. A lot of cruisers scoff at liveaboards, defined as those who live on their boat full time, a boat which may or may not actually move, or even have a motor for that matter. The reality of it is that a lot of potential cruisers are actually liveaboards that are continuing to work while they live on their boat at the dock, filling the cruising kitty, and getting the boat ready to cruise full time.

Deciding what kind of cruiser you're going to be will help you to choose the right boat and, by doing so, to greatly improve your chance of happiness and success with the venture. Will you figure it out on the first try? Maybe not, but thinking about it at all will help you to avoid owning one of the many sad, neglected boats that pepper the docks, moorings, and anchorages all over the common cruising grounds. Each of these boats tells a story of unrealized dreams, and putting a bit of thought and honest introspection into your style of cruising can help you avoid adding yours to the count. Here's our list of pros and cons for each kind of cruising. And yes, access to ice cream is a criterion for us.

Commuter Cruising

Pros	Cons
Time to visit family and friends	Expense of travel
Time to make money to cruise while on land	Added expense of two homes
Maintain government sponsored health care for Canadians	Added worries of maintenance for the off-season home

Marina Dwelling

Pros	Cons
Air conditioning in hot climates, heat in cold	Noise: other boats, road and city traffic, neighbors
Easy access to groceries, trash, water, electricity, laundry and sometimes (if you're lucky), wifi	Wifi rarely works
You get to meet more people	You have to put up with people you may not care for
Easier to work on the boat	Harder to go sailing since you're established in one place
Ice cream access is excellent	You spend *way* more money because things are so accessible
No need for a dinghy dock	Hard to get on and off the boat when the docks aren't floating docks. Easy to get hurt
	Power at the dock is sometimes low quality and can damage power cords and outlets (con't)

Pros	Cons
	Services vary widely for the same money.
	Wakes from passing boaters
	No running the generator – generators are rarely allowed in marinas

Mooring Ball Living

Pros	Cons
More stable ride since the boat always swings into the wind	Sometimes exposed
Good ventilation since the boat always swings into the wind	Sometimes relatively expensive and the quality is inconsistent
No worry about dragging anchor in high winds	You need to know the quality of the mooring and how frequently it is maintained
Access to services like groceries, banks, laundry, etc. depend on the facility	You spend more money the more accessible the services are
You can run the generator but...	If the moorings are close together some people get annoyed
Dinghy dock available, usually free	Wakes from passing boaters
Most mooring fields have cruiser nets to facilitate meeting other cruisers	For some reason jet skis feel it is their personal duty to run high speed through mooring fields
Ice cream access usually good	

Anchoring

Pros	Cons
Freedom. You rarely have anyone telling you what to do	You're totally responsible for your safety
You pick the view	Services vary depending on where you pick
Usually free	Harder to meet people
Anchoring well is a challenge and builds skill levels	Sometimes people can anchor too close or be obnoxious
Ventilation is good since the boat swings into the wind	Ice cream can be hit or miss
Did I mention free??	Dinghy docks are hard to come by and usually cost
4G internet available in most populated areas, even in the Bahamas	Wifi is rarely available without an extender and even with one most wifi is password protected
Privacy is excellent	
You can run the generator whenever you want	

When you think about these styles of cruising, compare them to what you know about yourself. What is your comfort level? Can you take harsh weather and rough seas on a mooring ball in an exposed mooring field? Are you a social butterfly that requires constant contact with friends and a schedule full of organized activities? What does your cruising kitty look like—will you need to work full time to pay for your cruising? Can you take a bath in a gallon and a half of water heated on the stove or do you require a 20 minute steamy shower? Can you sleep without air conditioning? All of these are questions that you must be totally honest in answering. It will go a long way toward choosing the right boat for your lifestyle.

Our boat, a 1982 Tartan 42, is a staunch blue water cruiser. She loves to have full sail up and bite into the waves at a 25° heel. Her cockpit is small so as not to fill up with more water than she can drain out before the next wave, her companionway is high and secure so as not to down-flood the cabin, her ports are sturdy and small so as not to break and leak in high seas, she is long and sleek and her beam is narrow, lending to speed. Sitting at anchor, though, we wish for a bigger cockpit with comfortable seating for entertaining and more storage so the aft cabin doesn't fill up like a storage shed. It would be nice to have an open companionway so a conversation could be carried on with the person in the galley below. It would also be great for vertically challenged crew to be able to see out the ports from a standing position in the boat. We're learning to deal with these issues, but we might have avoided them if we'd been able to determine what kind of cruisers we were going to be up front. What about you? Are you going to cruise the islands and spend most of your time snorkeling and fishing? Are you going to motor up and down the ICW? Or are you going to cross the Atlantic or sail around the world?

How capable are you of doing the work?

Not too many potential cruisers think about the work involved, in spite of the fact that a common cruising anecdote is that cruising is "boat maintenance in exotic locations." Just like dating, looking for a cruising boat will find you excited about all of the positive characteristics and ignoring all of the negative ones. The one thing that I realized after the first year of cruising is that it's a *lot* harder than I thought it was going to be. I've always been a hard worker, and I'm always working at something rather than sitting around, so it doesn't bother me as much as most. The level of work just to maintain and move a cruising boat can be overwhelming to many.

Here again, money is the key. If you have tons of it (bless your soul), you can always pay someone else to do the bulk of the work, but you better be watching over their shoulders because they won't be around when you're out in the middle of the Atlantic and the engine quits. If you're a budget cruiser like us, then you better be capable of doing all or most of your own work. I've been fortunate in this regard being married to a 40-year aircraft mechanic, I'm a decent mechanic myself, and we have the right tools, but a lot of people heading out have absolutely no mechanical inclination whatsoever. My advice? If you're not mechanically inclined, don't ever cruise out of range of Towboat US and buy an unlimited towing policy.

Other than mechanical issues, there is the constant parade of demands on your time like cleaning stainless, varnishing wood, lemon oiling interior teak, filling water tanks, doing laundry long distance or hand washing on the boat, groceries that take all day to buy, transport and stow, and all of the myriad of other daily chores that become all-day affairs on a cruising boat. Choosing your boat also has to reflect your capability of maneuvering in and on it. Our companionway steps are seven fairly steep steps and we must climb them dozens of times each day. Not the best choice if you have a bum knee. Getting in and out of the dinghy requires some dexterity as does moving around on deck. Navigating a side deck or fore-peak on nearly every sailboat can demand the skills of a gymnast. If balance or mobility is an issue, take care to think about that as you make your decisions.

Be honest with yourself about your capabilities. It's easy to say, "Oh, that won't be a problem" when you're in the thralls of a cruising dream and strolling around the Annapolis Strictly Sail displays, only to have your frustration derail the very same dream in the first few months of actual cruising.

How willing is your significant other?

It seems, from the reaction that we get, that most cruising dreams belong to the male in a conventional relationship. Our experience was the opposite. I had followed my husband around the country for 35 years chasing various forms of aviation employment, but it was my dream to live by the ocean. I'm very blessed to have a husband who cares very deeply for my happiness and was willing to tag along. He is also an adventurer, so it wasn't too hard to convince him, but he did sacrifice a good bit to make the voyage. He had to give up his motorcycle and his sports car, and he generally has a really hard time being away from the grandkids.

Someone recently put up a poll on the Women Who Sail Facebook group[1] asking the members if they thought that cruising could be successful if one or the other of the partners was unwilling. I answered that, in general, I don't believe it's possible. Clearly, there are those occasional relationships that work it out, but cruising is stressful enough without adding an unwilling partner to the mix. My experience is that

1 Women Who Sail is an excellent resource for information and camaraderie. It's a closed group so it's a good platform to ask questions without fear of reproach. It's also free to join. Just log into your Facebook account and search for Women Who Sail and request to join. Sorry guys, ladies only.

most of the abandoned cruising yachts for sale are a result of the unwilling partner stepping off the boat, buying a plane ticket, and going home, sometimes with a divorce attorney on speed dial. I have a good friend whose husband had the dream of cruising and she willingly went along but with no skills or preparation. She was overwhelmed early on but, through sheer grit and determination, has succeeded in becoming a comfortable and confident cruising spouse. I wholeheartedly admire her achievement but I find that most are not so strong-hearted.

In the event that a spouse is unwilling or unable to cruise, one solution we've seen multiple times is for the dreamer to single-hand commuter cruise. The dreamer cruises during the season, parking the boat somewhere in the islands for hurricane season, goes back home, and then returns to the boat for the next season. We have good friends doing this and it seems to work for them, but I would find it a very difficult life. It demands a stable, trusting relationship of two very independent people. Clearly, there must be very open communication between *any* cruising partners, but all the more so if one or the other is not as willing. One of the most remarkable examples of a solution to this difficulty was with another good friend of ours. He wanted to go cruising. She was less enthusiastic, but proposed up front to agree to five years after which they would re-evaluate their situation, with no argument if she wanted to return to land. They ended up cruising eight years, but have since returned to a land-based life to enjoy the accumulating grandchildren. When both partners are not mutually invested in the experience, clear and frequent communication is mandatory. The length of time cruising should be limited to a predefined period after which both partners will evaluate the experience and decide together if they will continue or move in another direction.

What are your expectations?

Expectations form the framework in which our experiences will live. Since cruising is a vastly different lifestyle than most of us live on land, knowing what to expect is sometimes difficult. Making it even more difficult is that it's sometimes hard to get an accurate picture of what cruising really *is* from people out there doing it because it's a different experience for different people. Ask 100 cruisers to define it and you'll get at least 50 answers. So how do you know what to expect? Read everything you can get your hands on and talk to every one you can.

In between reading books and blogs (see Chapter 2), take trips to marinas and talk to anyone who will talk to you on the dock. If you're land-locked, take vacations where you can visit marinas along the coast.

Cruising boats are pretty easy to spot. They usually have at least a half dozen jerry cans on deck for extra fuel and water and have laundry clipped to the line along with an assortment of sun shade covers in various sizes, colors and states of decay. If you take along a six-pack of your favorite craft beer you may even be invited on board for some more involved discussion.

Unrealistic expectations are a main cause for failure in many ventures, not just cruising. Set yourself up with people who will be honest with you, helping you to develop your expectations within reason so that when cruising exceeds those expectations you will be able to throw your arms to the sky and say, "Wow! Can you believe this?"

Can your cruising kitty support your expectations?

Finances are an extremely personal issue and as you prepare to cast off the dock lines, one of your greatest uncertainties will be the issue of cost. Because the lifestyle is so foreign to most preparing to go, there is literally no way to know how much money you will need to be comfortable without some advice from current cruisers. Fortunately, a lot of cruisers out there are willing to post their monthly expenditures for your perusal. While the reality of it is that you will spend whatever money you have available, you can get a feel for your requirements ahead of time by doing some math. Since we are both a bit detail-oriented, we had spreadsheets, something you may want to consider early on so that you have the ability to add and remove and change until you come up with a feasible budget for your cruising.

Tip →→ *For help with planning your cruising budget, visit the sidebar list "Costs of Cruising Links" on our cruising blog, The Retirement Project, www.theretirementproject.blogspot.com*

If you plan on spending any time at the dock or on mooring balls, dockage will be, without any doubt, your largest expense. In the first year of cruising we spent 170 days in marinas, 73 days on mooring balls, 120 swinging on an anchor, and the rest on overnight sails. We never planned on spending *any* time in marinas, but lack of experience and the travails of one of our children left us with no choice. If you don't think you'll be spending any time in marinas, think again, and plan your budget accordingly. Clearly, with more experience you could reduce those numbers, but having a nice, thick padding in the bank account will reduce your opportunities for failure due to the unexpected.

Depending on the age and size of the boat you purchase, boat maintenance will almost certainly be your next largest expense. It will not come regularly, but will come in huge chunks all at once and then none for a long while. This means that you must have savings set back that can accommodate that irregular timing. The general rule is that you will spend a minimum of 30-40% of the price you paid for your boat to get it outfitted for cruising, and then 10% of that purchase price per year to maintain it. This is not including any major refits down the road. It also largely depends on whether you will have someone else doing the work or whether you will do all or most of it yourselves. Our personal experience exceeded these amounts by far. Even doing all of the work ourselves, we have spent nearly 100% of the purchase price of the boat since we bought it and we still have a couple fairly major projects on the list. Is this unusual? Somewhat, but not as much as you would think. We run into cruisers all the time that do absolutely no maintenance on their boats at all. They are living in denial that will, with absolutely no doubt, catch up with them or, even worse, with the next owner which could be you. This is also about your tolerance level. We want to live in a nice home. We take care with small details like polishing brass and stainless, tending to both interior and exterior teak, polishing port lenses, and so forth. The two of us usually work a combined six or eight hours a day on boat chores with the associated expenses of cleaners, polishes, rags, varnish, etc.

For some, health care will be the next greatest expense. A lot of cruisers, especially young ones, were foregoing health insurance because they simply couldn't afford it, but with the new health care regulations in the United States that won't be an option. The hardest hit in this budget category are those like us: older cruisers who are just under the age of Medicare. Health insurance for this group is usually expensive and difficult to find. There are some groups like the Divers Alert Network (DAN) that offer some supplemental emergency health care assistance, as well as some travel policies if you're planning on cruising out of the country. In some countries it's simply cheaper to pay for your services with cash out of pocket. It is a topic of such complexity and confusion that it is outside the scope of this book. A lot of research information is out there for the taking. I will give one small example to help you in your decisions. We did not qualify for subsidized coverage under Obamacare because we had no income, only investments. This meant that we would be eligible for Medicaid except for the fact that Missouri opted out of Medicaid expansion so we were unable to qualify. All of the policies under Obamacare were prohibitively expensive (almost $1000 per month), so we went out and located one ourselves. We purchased private insurance through Anthem at $374 per month, with the one caveat: it had a very large deductible. We're generally healthy and we treated it as a catastrophic policy, accepting the risk. Early this year I had an irregular mammogram while we were back in St. Louis visiting family. While the results ended up benign, the costs of tests, doctors, anesthesiologists, and operating rooms ended up leaving us with an $10,500 hospital bill and an $11,000 deductible. As I mentioned before, these decisions are highly personal, but be prepared to accept whatever risk your decisions dictate.

Food and drink are next in the budget parade. Food expenses vary widely depending on whether you plan to cook all or most of your meals on board or whether you plan to eat out some or most of the time. Are you a connoisseur of fine dining, or are you satisfied with freshly caught fish and some macaroni and cheese? For some, alcohol and/or soda is a significant portion of the food bill, upwards of 30%. For others, water is all that's needed. Figure out how much you drink and budget it accordingly. Remember that you will probably drink more than you did on land and that you may need to allow for entertaining. Alcohol is a huge part of cruiser gatherings, so much so that some find it difficult to curtail. Allow 25-30% extra for food in the Bahamas. In the southern Caribbean, I'm told that there is a greater availability of locally grown produce at good prices, but the produce in the Bahamas is abysmal. It's always much more expensive, lower quality, and of unreliable stock. If you have a food you simply can't live without, buy it in the US and take it along. Just as an example, we saw bags of Doritos over there for $8.50 that would sell in the US for $3.79, and beer is never less than $3 a bottle.

Do your expectations include insurance? Most marinas require boat insurance and many require umbrella policies in the higher ranges. Will you want a towing service? Will you be staying in a hurricane zone year-round? Insurance can range anywhere from $1000 to $5000 for a typical 42-foot sailboat in the 20-30-year-old range and whatever your non-hurricane zone insurance is, your hurricane zone insurance will be double. A significant portion of the cruising community buys the mandatory liability insurance but has opted out of any hull insurance, taking their chances. For some, hull insurance is not even available. Very few marine insurance companies will insure a boat over 30 years old. Insurance is also a highly personal category. Each cruiser has to determine what their risk tolerance is and purchase accordingly.

$Tip \rightarrow \rightarrow$ *Before buying your cruising yacht, determine your insurance risk comfort level and talk to insurance agents about the insurability of your boat choice.*

Communications are next. Your communication habits and needs will determine how much you spend. If you're working from your boat you may spend as much as $400 per month just for internet access. Wifi is difficult to find, slower than molasses, usually password locked and unreliable at best, even with a wifi booster. Cell Internet is much more reliable and accessible but is limited and expensive. Are you a social butterfly? Do you cringe at the thought of being without Facebook? Budget the gigabytes or plan on sitting in Starbucks a lot. If you truly want to be off the grid and don't care about surfing the internet, then you can ignore this category altogether, but if you have families on land, or grandchildren like we do, communications will be a major player in your budget.

Power use of all sorts is a budget item to consider. You will have diesel for the inboard engine, gasoline for the dinghy motor, possibly gasoline for a Honda generator and possibly either propane or alcohol for cooking. Before we installed our solar panels, we averaged about 5 gallons of gasoline per week for the generator and dinghy combined at our maximum power use and an average of two dinghy trips per day. Since installing our solar (255 watts), our gasoline consumption has been cut by about 60%. Solar and wind are initial outlays that require very little maintenance, so clearly they are a good investment if you can afford the up-front expense. Solar costs are going down exponentially every year and the performance is increasing at about the same rate. If you plan on marina stays, a minimum power charge is almost always added to your rate, even if you don't plan on using any. More and more marinas are charging a mandatory "utilities" fee which covers water, power, and pump-out.

I've always handled the budget in our marriage and I'm quite picky about pennies so I had a pretty good handle on what our expenses were going to be. We'd lived aboard the boat in our home marina for 3-4 days a week for over three years which gave us a good idea of our food/water/power/fuel/pump-out requirements. In spite of this, there were a few surprises for us.

I greatly underestimated the cost of doing laundry while cruising. I enjoy hand-washing when we're in the Bahamas because we have the time to do it and abundant sunshine to dry it, but hand-washing in the city anchorages in the USA is something we try to avoid, mostly because we try very hard to respect the view of the homeowners on shore by not hanging our "tidy whities" on our lifelines. There is a growing animosity toward liveaboards in the States, especially in Florida, and we try always to extend the courtesy we would want if it were our expensive property the boat was parked in front of. Laundry in the States runs anywhere from $1.50 to wash and $1.50 to dry to upwards of $5.00 each in the Bahamas. As cruisers are wont to do, we wear everything at least several days, and yet we still average a load a week.

Ice was another underestimated expense. I confess to being a typical US-of-A cold-drink addict. I like my water cold enough that it almost hurts going down. We keep a Thermos jug on our counter which we fill with ice water in the morning for the day. We also have developed a rather nasty predilection for mocha frappes, a habit developed because we happen to have a Magic Bullet on board and really like iced coffee. We have a very good refrigerator which will freeze meat and keep it frozen if you lay it right on the plate, but it won't freeze enough ice for us and it won't keep ice cream frozen, so we buy ice in 10# bags when we can get it and we average one every few days when it's really hot and we're drinking a lot of iced coffee.

If you're good at it, bartering can go a long way to funding your cruising. It is incredibly common for cruisers to exchange work for work or work for food or alcohol. If you have a trade skill that cruisers want, like electrical talent or an ability as a diesel mechanic, you will be able to trade that for things you need. We have a good friend who spent $1500 for a whole year of cruising because he found most of what he needed in and around dumpsters behind boat yards, ran his engine on used cooking oil that he picked up for free from restaurants, and traded work for food. He is highly talented and creative, but he worked nearly the hours of a full-time job doing it, and many potential cruisers are not interested in a full-time job. I did recently read an article about a guy who earns over $240,000 a year by dumpster diving behind retail establishments and then selling the stuff on eBay. Like I said, it can be done, but most cruisers left the life of consuming behind and want only to live simply.

Monthly cruising budgets can range anywhere from a few hundred dollars for someone in a 22-foot engineless sailboat living on Ramen noodles, to over $100,000 and beyond for a large cruising yacht with a gourmet chef. Determining where you fit in that scale, and what your comfort level is, will be one of the most difficult decisions you will make. As much as we like to think we're living an off-grid lifestyle and that we've shunned the world of excess, it still takes money to get by, and determining how much you need to be comfortable is essential.

If we had it to do over again (they *do* say that hindsight is 20/20), we would have sold the condo much earlier, moved into a rental studio apartment, and saved every dime we could. Approaching it this way would have given us more practice living in a small space and would have dramatically reduced our spending and increased our savings. We've done alright, but it would be nice to have the extra cushion.

So if, after thinking honestly about all of these things, you still want to be a cruiser, read on. While sometimes frightening, it's an exciting and fulfilling journey to realize your dreams.

2 GETTING YOUR FEET WET
(Blogs & Websites, Books, Classes, Charters)

The process of deciding to adopt a cruising lifestyle evolves differently for each person, but almost always involves copious amounts of reading. Reading is an excellent way to get a feel for the lifestyle and to try to determine how you can fit into it.

Blogs & Websites

Reading about cruising has been made much easier with the proliferation of sailing blogs in recent years. Early on in our planning I found about 20 blogs that I followed in my Feedly[2] reader. I chose them carefully and for different reasons. Some I chose because the boat featured was one similar to what we wanted. Some I chose because the people were in similar situations as we were in or had similar temperaments. Some I chose because their cruising grounds were places we wanted to explore. Over the years I dropped some and added others because the blogs and our needs were constantly changing, but I always followed about 20 of them. Even after going cruising, and with limited internet access, I still follow a half dozen or so cruising blogs. Don't be afraid to contact the blog writers if you have specific questions. I've yet to run across one who wasn't happy to converse with you via email to help you get started. It does require some patience as a lot of cruisers are out of internet range for long stretches at a time, but the wait will be worth it. We all had people do the same for us at some point so we're happy to help others.

There are literally thousands of cruising blogs out there. Google "cruising sailing blog" and you'll get 1,300,000 results. Again, at the risk of omitting many really great blogs, here is a list of some of the ones that were on my list of 20, most of whom have been mentors and patiently answered a multitude of questions.

---

2 The Feedly reader is a great way to keep up with a lot of blogs. Go to www.feedly.com and sign up for free. Then add as many blogs as you want to follow (www.theretirementproject.blogspot.com would be a great one to start with).

zerotocruising.com	Mike and Rebecca on a PDQ32 catamaran, now transitioning to their own charter boat. Rebecca also has a good boat fitness blog, strengthplus.ca.
sailingtotem.com	Behan Gifford and her family aboard a Stephens 47. She is also active in the Women Who Sail Facebook group.
sailfarlivefree.com	Kevin and his family aboard a Catalina 34. This blog is a fantastic resource for all things sailing.
bumfuzzle.com	Pat and Ali and kids. This family quit cruising and now blogs about cruising in an RV. It's an excellent foray into reasons for stopping the cruising life.
windtraveler.net	Brittany and Scott and 3 kids aboard their Brewer 44. Lots of good insight and honesty here.
therebelheart.com	Eric and Charlotte and 2 kids, now on land after a disastrous scuttling of their boat in the Pacific. Gritty honesty.
svthirdday.com	Rich and Lori and kids on a Hudson Force 50. Good blog about running a business from a boat and where to find the best tacos.
veranda422.blogspot.com	Bill and Christy now on land. Our most gracious mentors as we prepared to go cruising. A good source of technical information with humor.
tendervittles.net	Tom and Amy on a PDQ 36 living in Georgetown. A good source of what daily life is like in the islands with a hilarious sense of humor thrown in.

morganscloud.com	This reference blog, authored by John and Phyllis and some guest commentators is a wealth of knowledge for new cruisers.
zachaboard.blogspot.com	A great live-aboard blog about life on a boat with kids. Good source for homeschooling info.
commutercruiser.com	One of the few, if not the only, cruising blogs dedicated to life as a commuter cruiser.
boatbits.blogspot.com	A blog with some refreshing random thoughts on things boat related and not boat related.
panbo.com	All things electronic and new gadgetry written by Ben Ellison.
sailfeed.com	A good resource site that also has a group of blogs it publishes. If your time is limited then this one site is a good place to start.
pbase.com/mainecruising	One of the most comprehensive how-to sites available. Step-by-step pictures with detailed instructions on how to do many things on a boat like rebedding things and rebuilding a winch.

I've found that there are several general types of cruising blogs. There are the resource/instructional blogs like morganscloud.com, panbo.com, sailfarlivefree.com, etc., whose information is easy to fact check, are usually highly professional and greatly beneficial. A tremendous amount can be learned from these blogs even after you leave to go cruising. Blogs like panbo can be excellent technical resources when you're looking to upgrade or purchase new equipment.

There are log-style blogs that detail daily living with very little philosophical commentary. Some are for the author's use as a ship's log, or for detailing the day to family back home, and can go a long way to

21

letting you see what a typical day in the life of a cruiser involves. I generally don't read many of the log-style blogs because they often descend into a Facebook-style "I went to the store and I did laundry and I hung out" list of mundane tasks that are only of interest to the writer. The only one of these blogs that I picked for my Feedly Reader was tendervittles.net, which is a cross between a log-style and journal-style blog. I chose it because the author, Tom, paints his day with a hilarious sense of very dry humor which consistently makes me laugh and I happen to believe that no cruiser will be successful without a sense of humor.

The most common type of blog is a journal style of writing where useful technical information and project reports are mixed with personal observations and photos. Most of the other blogs on my list (as well as our own blog) fall into this category. These blogs will be colored by the authors' willingness to be honest with themselves, and whatever view of the cruising lifestyle they have chosen to present. Some authors simply do not want to say anything if they don't have anything good to say and, while this is an admirable trait in personal relationships, it doesn't present an accurate picture of what the cruising lifestyle is for potential cruisers. You may be different, but I want to know the complete story before making a major life-changing decision. If it's common to have to use a bucket because you're fixing the stinky leak from the head and can't find parts, I'd like to know this before selling my house with three bathrooms and a plumber on call.

Blogs can be a mixed blessing. If they are presenting an unrealistic picture of the cruising life, they can leave you unprepared for the sometimes difficult realities of cruising. If they are too dire, you run the risk of being afraid to try, afraid to risk the chance to reap rewards the likes of which you've never experienced. We struggle daily on our blog to balance the need to be honest about our difficulties and challenges with the need to stress the phenomenal benefits that we've received. Over the two years since we left, our lives have swelled from high to low to high many times, and we believe the blog reflects that. I guess it's fitting to use the analogy of waves. Your cruising life will certainly travel from the peak of one to the valley of the next. If you choose a blog to read, please read it over a long stretch of time to give the author the chance to reflect these highs and lows. You can generally get a good feel for a blog by looking back in its archives and by paying attention to comments left.

Books

As far as conventional books go, there are a few worthy of mention and I do so at the peril of omitting others, but I'll do it anyway. This is in no way an inclusive list, just a list of some of the ones I've personally read and enjoyed and found helpful.

Title	Author
The Voyager's Handbook: The Essential Guide to Blue Water Cruising	Beth Leonard
The Annapolis Book of Seamanship	John Rousmaniere
How Boat Things Work	Charlie Wing
Marine Diesel Engines	Nigel Calder
Sailing a Serious Ocean	John Kretschmer
Sailing Fundamentals	Gary Jobson
The Cost Conscious Cruiser	Lin and Larry Pardey
Complete Illustrated Sailboat Maintenance Manual	Don Casey
World Cruising Routes	Jimmy Cornell
Heavy Weather Sailing	K. Adlard Coles
Sensible Cruising:The Thoreau Approach	Don Casey
Used Boat Notebook	John Kretschmer
Maiden Voyage	Tania Aebi

Title	Author
An Embarrassment of Mangoes	Ann Vanderhoof
At the Mercy of the Sea	John Kretschmer
The Long Way	Bernard Moitessier
The 12-Volt Bible for Boats	Edwin Sherman and Miner Brotherton
Boatowners Mechanical and Electrical Manual	Nigel Calder
The Everything Knots Book	Randy Penn
Emergency Navigation	David Burch
Alexander and the Terrible, Horrible, No Good, Very Bad Day	Judith Viorst – If you've owned a boat before, you'll understand why this children's book is listed. A sense of humor is required to cruise.

Classes

Reading books, and visiting blogs and websites can be a great way for you to begin to see if this is something you really want to do. Ditching your old stuff-filled life for one of cruising is a major lifestyle change and beginning to think about it as a possibility for yourself is a bit like trying on a new outfit to see if it fits. Blogs and websites can be a terrific beginning to set the stage in your mind, to get a feel for the atmosphere and to see if you think your personality will be suitable, but eventually you have to get out there and get your feet wet. Classes give you a chance to get out there and try cruising, to learn something while you're at it, and to do it without an excessive amount of financial risk.

The day after dropping the retirement idea bomb on my husband, I made a call to the St. Louis Sailing Center. After arming us with some very helpful information, the folks there had us registered for our first sailing class of the ASA-101 variety and had class books in the mail to us. Being the ever-so-diligent students that aviation seems to produce, we eagerly awaited their arrival so we could bone up before class. We'd never even been on a sailboat before and we had a *lot* to learn.

If you're in the growing group of wanna-be cruisers who, like us, had never been on a sailboat before, then taking a couple sailing classes from a reputable school is a very wise thing to do. It's good to know which end of a sailboat is which. Besides, at least you'll be able to impress your non-sailing guests with your salty knowledge of lines and cleats and knots and starboard and port rather than fumbling around and yelling, "Grab that rope—the dirty one that used to have red stripes on it—the one on the right!" Sailing courses vary widely in their cost and effectiveness, but if you stick with American Sailing Association (ASA) courses[3] then the material will be standardized. Instructors also vary widely and the instructor that is effective with you may not be effective with your friend. We were fortunate to end up with an instructor that met our learning style for our ASA-101 and ASA-103 courses, a woman who allowed us the freedom to explore and ask questions and basically teach ourselves with supervision, a learning style which works well for us. I've heard of other instructors with a military bent that ran highly structured courses. Not for us, but some may need the structured discipline. We were also fortunate that St. Louis Sailing Center was using a cruising boat for their classes at the time. We took our 101 and 103 classes on a new-ish Catalina 310, a good weekend cabin boat, and we were able to visualize ourselves "out there" because of the boat we were on. Had we taken the course on the Colgate 26s that they currently use, I can't honestly say we would have been as enthusiastic. There may be some merit to taking a sailing course with someone like Blue Water Sailing School[4] in Ft. Lauderdale that uses full-sized cruising boats and sails in waters that cruisers frequent. You will find as many opinions on this issue as you will cruisers. Some say that you should learn to sail on small boats like the Laser, and that you should participate in club racing because it will teach you to be a better sailor. I've done both, and while they were good experiences, they did absolutely nothing to prepare me for the cruising experience.

Taking ASA classes is a great way to gain the basic knowledge you need if you're completely new to sailing. We did take the beginning ASA classes and the knowledge that we gained there was invaluable as an introduction. The most effective training we had, however, was not an ASA course at all, but a blue water training voyage offered by

---

3   For more information on ASA courses you can contact them directly on their website, www.asa.com or you can search Google for schools that offer their courses. Talk to people at your local marinas to get a feel for the courses and instructors at each school to determine what might be the best match.

4   You can contact Blue Water Sailing School via their website, www.bwss.com.

John Kretschmer Sailing[5] out of Ft. Lauderdale, FL. John's voyages allow you to go sailing with a highly experienced sailor/cruiser and learn as much or as little as you want. He is a soft-spoken, capable sailor that quit counting his sea miles somewhere in excess of 350,000. He is passionate about the sea, a passion that you can't help but acquire when you sail on *Quetzal*. Some of his courses, like his heavy weather training voyage, are not for the faint of heart, but the Bahamas Bash that runs from Ft. Lauderdale to the Bahamas and back is an excellent one for beginners. His voyages are fairly expensive, but the voyage we took was the best training dollars we spent. He also runs a cruiser university once a year in the fall in Annapolis. I've never attended, but he does an intensive 4-day class on what to expect when you take off in your own cruising boat.

Be careful what schools you use and do your research on the boat involved. We had a very unfortunate experience with a school that will remain unnamed. The boat was a maintenance disaster and we were fortunate to get through the week without ending up using the dinghy for a life raft. We learned a lot that week, but the risk/reward ratio was heavily skewed against us.

The first day of ASA-101 was a classroom day where we were hit with an overwhelming list of sailing terms and parts of the boat. And yes, there will be a test at the end. It was a Friday night class that let out late and was followed with two days in the boat on the lake. The lake being Lake Carlyle situated 60 miles East of our home in St. Louis, and us being the aforementioned aviation-trained students of the dedicated variety, we were the first to arrive by a good bit. But we had a thermos of hot coffee in tow and the boat was not locked behind a gate, so we plopped ourselves in the cockpit and smiled at each other. You know, that ahhhhh-this-is-definitely-not-a-cubicle-smile. I knew then that our lives going forward would be defined by this moment.

Our two days of ASA-101 class were uneventful, so much so that even the wind forgot to attend. We still had a great time getting to know our fellow students, learning how to work the boat and, in the occasional brief gust of breeze, even sailing a bit. Even with the lack of excitement, we were smitten and were counting the days to the 103 course.

By the time we had gotten to our ASA-105 and 106, we were tired of schools. As pilots, we've both had to take uncountable numbers of classes and taken as many government tests. We were getting

5   You can find John Kretschmer Sailing at www.yayablues.com. His courses are usually booked out more than one year so plan ahead. They are also not cheap, so plan ahead. He is an accomplished author and his books are available on amazon.com for an entertaining read when you're stuck inside by the fireplace in the winter.

comfortable with sailing, knew most of the basic concepts and terminology, and had enough background to be able to go on and teach ourselves. Since the particular course that involved the 105 and 106 curriculum happened to be the Pearson 35 disaster, there ended up not being enough time to take the tests at the end of the week trip. We were given 12 months to study and take the test, but we decided not to do it. We had learned the material and we had absolutely no need to prove anything to anyone else.

Sailing schools are one way to get there, but they may not be the answer for you. For us, time was a factor. We weren't getting any younger and didn't feel we had the time to spend learning how to sail in a yacht club or from friends. Taking the ASA classes and the training voyage with John Kretschmer was a fast-track way to get enough knowledge and experience for us to make a decision as to whether we really liked the lifestyle and wanted to continue a track to the goal of cruising. If you're younger and have the luxury of learning at a slower pace, then a yacht club with a racing program may be a good way for you to get the experience you need.

If you are one of the previously mentioned inexperienced spouses following a dreamer, there are quite a few schools out there for ladies only, with female instructors. Since I've never attended one, I can't recommend any particular courses, but you can do an internet search and find several dozen of them. Just do your homework and read the reviews before committing your cash. For more information and reviews, you can utilize the massive amount of knowledge and experience that is available through the Facebook group Women Who Sail.

Tip →→ *Travel insurance is a wise purchase to protect your investment dollars for classes and charters.*

Whatever classes you elect to take, be sure to purchase travel insurance. If the weather goes bad or the boat becomes unavailable due to maintenance, or you become ill, it can save your hard-earned investment. Most of these classes are in the $2,000-4,000 range and are non-refundable. Many of them are also in storm-prone areas. It's easy to have the class trip called off and leave you stranded with an airline ticket you can't use and a deposit lost. You can get a good travel insurance policy for just a couple hundred dollars, and most of them include emergency medical transportation and/or coverage supplemental to your own health care coverage. Our ASA-114 catamaran course was so modified due to an usual tropical storm in the Gulf that year. We were scheduled to leave Pensacola Beach and go outside the cut to Panama City, but the storm kept us in the bay behind the barrier islands. We didn't object, because the school extended our class to 9 days instead of 6 to compensate for the days we couldn't sail, and living on the catamaran for 9 days was a treat for us.

A word about cost here: sometimes schools can be the best value. The class we took advertised that it was one-on-one instruction so we had the catamaran to ourselves. The instructor came in the morning and was gone by 4:30 each day. We had the boat all to ourselves the remainder of the time. Had we chartered a Lavezzi 40 we would have spent at least twice as much for the same 9 days on a private boat.

Charters

Early on, before we decided to take the classes we took, we considered the possibility of chartering in order to gain experience. We had several groups of people in our home yacht club who took charter trips at least twice a year and invited us to go along. Chartering can be a great way to build experience, but it didn't seem to be the best fit for us.

Since we didn't have enough experience to charter a boat by ourselves, we would have had to go in a group, most likely with other members of our yacht club. For those of you who have never been on a boat in close quarters with friends, it can be somewhat challenging. A boat is a very small space, and habits that didn't bother you about someone on land can be quite difficult to ignore in the 400 square feet of most charter boats. One thing we learned quickly was that there are as many sailing styles as there are sailors, and what works for one is not necessarily the best for the next. Our ability to learn would have depended greatly on who was the captain on any given charter. We wanted to remain good friends with the members of our yacht club and we realized that we needed to find our own way to make our dream happen, so we felt chartering was not necessarily the best use of our training funds, which were limited.

Whether you choose to do your hands-on training through classes or chartering, it's important to remember that while they will give you the benefits of learning about different types of boats and how they might fit you, neither of those will give you a true idea of what it's like to be out there cruising. On either a class boat or a charter boat you have very little responsibility for maintenance, especially the sort that seems to pop up at the most inconvenient times. If your budget will be restricted it's not likely that you will have the funds to purchase the newer type of boat that most charter companies or schools supply. Use classes and charters to give you general background, but if you have an opportunity to go spend a week or two with someone out there actually cruising, the opportunity is gold. It will provide you with a real-world look into the lifestyle and hopefully some long, honest discussions over sundowners in the cockpit.

Some charter companies are run by long-time cruising couples or families and they can be a good compromise. A good example would be Bahamas Cat Charters, a company run by a friend of ours (www.bahamascatcharters.com). They have been cruising for more years than they can count, have circumnavigated, and raised their sons on board. Their sons are now running their own boats in the company.

Notes

3 TRAINING WHEELS
(Your First Learning Boat)

There I was, sitting in my favorite chair and reading the latest issue of "Rider" magazine. Out of nowhere, my wife of many decades leans over the stair railing and asks, "What do you think about retiring onto a boat?" Clearly she was suffering from some kind of hallucination, or maybe I was having a dream. Retire onto a boat? Retire? Boat? What in the world was she talking about?

I was a pilot and a long distance motorcyclist. So was she. My first solo flight happened within a few weeks of my sixteenth birthday. I had been sneaking rides on dirt bikes and mini-bikes, owned by friends, years before that. I got to ride in exchange for keeping the things running. During an aviation career that spanned forty years, I had been a Maintenance Manager, Charter Captain, line pilot on a commuter airline, and a Director of Flight Operations. There had been a few years spent on an airshow team where low-level acrobatics in an all-out, performance-based single-seat beast of an airplane had been near-daily exercises. During those years we had done several things in airplanes that had never been done before and, maybe, will never be done again. I had flown as an airline Captain in 80-passenger regional jets in and out of some of the busiest airports on the planet in all kinds of weather. That, by the way, is the Super Bowl for professional aviators, and it is much more work than the airlines want anyone to suspect. At the moment my wife leaned over that railing, my job was Corporate Flight Department Manager, hauling the Big-Wigs around the country in a company jet.

The many motorcycles that spent time in my garage usually leaned toward the "go fast" end of the spectrum. And, in my mind anyway, if one owns a motorcycle that was built to go fast, one should go fast on it. Triple digit runs were not uncommon. Once, while riding back from a little airport, it started to snow. It occurred to me that I had never ridden over 100 mph in the snow, so I did, just for the sheer hell of it. That bike, a BMW K1200RS, had heated hand grips and an excellent fairing, so it wasn't as cold a ride as it was when I did the same on my last bike, a Suzuki GSXR1000. Retire onto a boat? Other than going fishing with my grandfathers when I was a kid, I couldn't remember ever being on a boat. Well, motorcycle rides sometimes included a ride across a river or lake on a ferry. Did that even count?

On the other hand, I had just turned 50 years old. When I dared think about it, my days of running deep into triple digit speeds and then braking hard for the next corner, diving in and dragging a knee around the apex, were clearly numbered. I had survived many years of running bikes just about as hard as they could be run on the street, and had never been badly hurt. Bikes and airplanes had surely used up more than my allotted nine lives.

But more importantly to me, it was simply Deb's turn. She had followed me back and forth across the country while I took jobs I wanted, just for the experience and risk. Flying air ambulance in the Rocky Mountains and then the airshow team forced her to leave friends she loved and places she knew. My oldest daughter had done high school in four different time zones. Having a rush junkie as a husband or father is not an easy calling. If my long-suffering wife wanted to explore retiring onto a boat, then that is what we would do.

Our first weekend class on a Catalina 310 sealed the deal. I was all in. After our second weekend class on that same Catalina it was clear that this "retiring early onto a sailboat" had become our newest obsession. We set an arbitrary 5 year goal of making it happen. Selling everything that wouldn't fit on a boat while saving and investing enough money to actually retire were serious obstacles. But to me, the biggest challenge was actually learning how to operate and maintain a boat big enough and complex enough to live on. One that would include a cabin, maybe some kind of air conditioning and heating system, water system, waste water system, some way to keep and cook food, DC and AC electrical systems with batteries and chargers. There would be some kind of engine to drive the boat and all of its related systems: propeller, shaft, transmission, fuel, cooling, and oil. Since it would be a sailboat, all of the associated masts, sails, boom, lines, clutches, winches, vangs, and blocks that were still mostly a mystery to me would need mastered. And don't forget anchors and chains, snubbers and windlasses.

Right here is where the first bit of reality intersected with the dream. Sooner or later, if a person is actually going to live on a boat, well, that person will actually have to buy a boat and live on it. And if that same person actually wants to learn how to sail, eventually he (or she) will have to point the skinny end of a boat out toward the water where the waves are running and the wind is blowing and make it happen. We were in need of a "starter boat."

The very idea of us buying a boat was a bit scary. It shouldn't have been. By then we had owned several houses, cars, motorcycles, and even a couple of little airplanes. How big a deal could buying a sailboat be?

A C&C Mega 30 on the hard at Tradewinds, the marina where our classes had been based, was the first to catch our eye. But it didn't seem quite right. Designed to ride on a trailer, it was crowded inside, dark, and cave-like. A lifting keel filled much of the space, and the boat was simply beat. The first boat we looked at we walked away from without looking back. It was a habit we should have honed to a much sharper edge.

There were three other marinas at Lake Carlyle to explore. One of them was home base for serious racers and their open-hulled speed machines. Having cut my "go-fast" teeth on 160MPH sport bikes and making inverted passes close to the ground at nearly 200 mph in the show plane, racing sailboats just didn't make a lot of sense. (Still doesn't.)

Marina number three was just too pricey. Dock fees were the highest on the lake, as was the club membership. Boats for sale were the nicest, newest, and by far the most expensive. One or two of them would have been acceptable as "the boat" for coastal or ICW sailors, but we were just getting started. We were honest enough to admit that, while this seemed a thing we wanted to do now, there was no promise of it being a thing we wanted to do after learning a bit more. Buying one of these boats would have been a serious, life-altering commitment all by itself. We were not there yet.

"Starter boat" is a good description. This boat will be the one where the limited space, constant motion, continuous need to keep an eye on the weather and surrounding conditions, and limited access to creature comforts will start to become apparent. On this boat, modern life's insatiable need for electricity will start to rear its ugly head. It is where the amount of trash generated starts to fill the boat with smells, and where the smells that people generate start to be unavoidable.

The starter boat is the one where noises begin to be overwhelmingly important. What is that creak? What is that groan? Is the boat dragging on its anchor, banging against the dock, taking on water? That sizzling noise—are those really shrimp? It sounds like the boat is on fire. (Saltwater newbies.) What is that thumping on the hull? (Carp, for those on inland waters.)

The starter boat is the one used to determine whether cruising is a real, workable goal, or a dream best left as a dream. If cruising turns out to be a dream and not a goal, then the starter boat becomes the bail-out boat. And herein lies a problem. A starter boat needs to teach the things needing taught: systems, living aboard, anchoring out, sailing a cabin, living on the water. This is not necessarily a small boat, nor is it particularly inexpensive. It will likely need dock space, insurance and maintenance. Depending on where it is located it may need hauled in the off-season and stored. And if the discovery is that cruising and sailing are really not the goal after all, it will need to be sold. Until it is, the bills keep coming in. A bail-out boat needs to be cheap.

A careful review of our financial situation suggested that having a "yacht" floating at a pier somewhere, even a modest one old enough to buy beer and needing some work, would be a reach. We were looking for cheap, but we also needed to learn.

Boulder Marina was on the far side of the lake as seen from St. Louis, adding 20 minutes to the commute. We rode in to look at a Catalina 27 floating at the dock. Deb went down the companionway and started forward. I climbed into the cockpit and started forward. We met at the hatch in the v-berth, exchanged the look long time couples have for "lets get out of here" and walked quickly away. Neither of us were sure why the thing was still floating.

Since we were at a marina we decided to go exploring, walking the docks and chatting with some of those sitting in cockpits and enjoying a beautiful day. We shared that we were looking to buy a boat because "we were going cruising." Instead of being laughed off the premises we were pointed to a ComPac 27 sitting shrink-wrapped on her cradle. The owner was aboard getting the boat ready to sell, though he had yet to officially list it. We were welcomed up the ladder. A few weeks later my much-loved BMW K1200RS went out the door to make financial room, and little *Nomad* joined the family.

Nomad was a perfect starter boat. She was big enough for the two of us to live on for days at a time, with near stand-up room in the cabin for me. There was a galley, head, water systems, electrical systems; in fact, everything I needed to learn to operate and maintain. Better yet she was a tough little thing that shrugged off all of our early mistakes learning to make a sailboat go. In addition, she had been a kind of "hobby boat" for her previous owner, and was exceptionally well maintained...for a boat.

I had been operating and maintaining aircraft all of my life. "Maintain," in my case, meant the actual laying on of tool-wielding hands. In addition to being a pilot, I am a certified aircraft mechanic and inspector. As a boat owner, that turned out to be both a blessing and a curse.

The first boat I ever drove onto a dock was *Nomad*. Riding in the boat as the travel lift carried her to the water, all I could think of was the boat going straight under the moment the lift set us free. Nothing like that happened of course. The engine fired on the first try, the broker stood next to me giving lessons, and we got the boat to the dock with little fanfare. It would be a while before things went that smoothly again.

34

A couple of weekends of cleaning things up and figuring things out past, it was time to try out this sailing thing. Deb wanted to take someone along for the first voyage. I figured we had already taken two classes and insisted that we give it a go on our own.

As *Nomad* eased out of the slip the wind caught her stern, pushing it the wrong way. That I had forgotten to ease off of the helm brake and then turned the wrong direction after I did get it free, didn't help. We ended up bow pointed toward the dead-end part of the causeway instead of out toward the lake. People on shore clapped and cheered, I think because we didn't hit anything. A second try, this time listening to what Deb was saying about which way to turn the helm, and we were pointed out toward the big, open water of tiny Lake Carlyle.

We decided to motor across the lake to Tradewinds, the idea to show our new boat to new friends. Two thirds of the way across the lake smoke started pouring out of the engine compartment. Engine fire to a pilot is an instant, life-and-death challenge. My brain went into overdrive trying to come up with some kind of checklist to run. Shutting down the engine was obvious, but now we were just floating and completely out of control. (At all of about 2 knots.) What to do? Deb suggested we toss out the anchor, get a beer, and think about it. Emergency over.

Friends from Tradewinds towed us in. We spent the night at the fuel dock and the next morning I fiddled with the cooling system. It seemed to work better so off toward home base we went. The winds were light to non-existent but we hung a sail out anyway and shut off the engine. A few hours later we had mostly drifted close enough to start the engine and try for the dock. I don't remember hitting anything too hard, and our first weekend "out on the boat" was deemed a qualified success.

The next weekend was the Fourth of July, a serious party at Lake Carlyle. On Saturday night rafts of boats gather together to watch the fireworks display at the south end of the lake. There is a bit of a contest over which of the three "cruiser boat" marinas has the most boats tied together. *Nomad* was going to be part of the Boulder showing.

Winds were gusting to 25 plus as we cleared into the lake. Main and jib were deployed and *Nomad* picked up her skirts and danced toward the dam. Several times she leaned over hard, the helm went dead under my hands and then the boat spun up into the wind and stopped. That, I thought, was pretty cool. The boat was obviously designed with some kind of "auto-brake" thing in mind. How much trouble could a person get into if the boat stopped itself if pushed too hard?

A few hours later we were the last to arrive at the raft-up. That was deliberate since I did not want to be in the middle of the pack. The rest of the group was a bit unnerved at the sight of *Nomad* approaching with me at the helm. People drifted to our expected landing spot with boat hooks and fenders, which I took as a welcoming gesture from our new friends. With all that help it was easy to slide into place where we got our first lesson in tying a group of boats together. Sitting in our cockpit enjoying a cold one, a soon to be life-long friend joined us.

"I saw you sailing down the lake this afternoon. *Nomad* was looking good but you might think about reefing the sail next time. It looked like you were carrying too much canvas for the wind."

My brain was stuck at "reefing," with not a clue what he meant. That evening, after the fireworks and the party wound down, I got on the internet to search "reefing a sailboat." Sailing home the next morning, in even more wind, was much, much easier.

That set the tone for our next few seasons. In addition to *Nomad* being a wonderful teacher, our home base was a marina full of serious sailors. People who became close friends were also seasoned charter sailors and racers. Just some of the parts of the world they had explored under sail included most of the Bahama and Caribbean Islands, the Gulf of Mexico, and parts of the Mediterranean Sea. By the time we started thinking of replacing *Nomad* with "The Boat," she was a pretty well-sorted little lake boat. We had learned to keep her systems, including the temperamental 2 cylinder, 9HP diesel, running and happy.

In addition, we had earned the reputation for being among the first people to head out when the winds picked up, and the last to head in. One of the highest compliments I have ever gotten came from one of those life-long friends and experienced sailors. "You," he said one day "can make a slow boat go fast."

The last season with *Nomad* may still be some of the best times we have had on a boat. Most weekends we would leave the dock on Friday afternoon and not return until late Sunday evening. Night sailing was normal and anchoring in our favorite cove second nature. We dodged or rode out some serious thunderstorms, made good decisions about when to be bold and when to run and hide, and no one reached for a boat hook when we eased up to the weekend raft-up. The ComPac 27 was a stout, easily sailed boat with tough bones. Indeed, Nomad's new owner took her out west where, last we heard, she was happily romping around the San Francisco Bay.

In retrospect, we might have made one serious mistake with *Nomad*, selling her too soon. It may have been better if we had stayed with her for the first part of our cruising life. In our case that meant trucking her to the Chesapeake Bay and sailing, mostly down the ICW, to Florida. Truth to tell, if she had been a ComPac 35 instead of a 27, that is exactly what would have happened. So consider buying a starter boat that is just capable enough to start your cruising life with. (Unless, of course, you imagine yourself heading straight out across an ocean.) The first boat is never going to be the right boat. There is too much that can't be learned until after the dock lines fall away from a home port for that last time. But the more you learn about what you need before trading up to "the boat," the better that boat will fit your needs.

Little *Nomad* and an exceptional group of sailors and friends, had taught us about everything we could learn about sailing and living aboard a small inland lake. It was time to consider moving on.

Notes

4 THE AFFLICTION WITH NO CURE
(Or, "Honey take a look at this one!")

Prior to the advent of the internet, if you wanted to buy a boat you had to get on the phone and contact brokers in your area to see what boats were available. They could mail you

Kintala's yachtworld.com ad

pictures but, because of the cost associated, they were usually a rather sparse collection. Generally you bought whatever was close to you because looking far away was just too hard and cost prohibitive.

With the dawn of the internet age came yachtworld.com, sailboatlistings.com and boattrader.com, just to name a few. Internet speeds increased exponentially every year so uploading 40 or 50 or 70 pictures into your boat ad was no problem. All of a sudden, the boat market became a national, or even international one if you were hell-bent on buying a particular model. The person that bought our first boat, *Nomad*, came all the way from Idaho to Illinois because he had his heart set on a Compac 27 and had found ours on sailboatlistings.com.

Boat shopping online is addicting. Ask any person currently looking for a boat or any person who has recently purchased one and you'll either get a flat denial, a horribly underestimated count of hours or a sheepish grin. Why is it so addicting? It's the same as any other addiction: it offers escape.

I found myself sitting in front of the computer for hours on end in the evenings, pouring over countless ads of boats that we couldn't even remotely afford, imagining our lives in them. The key here? Imagining. Absolutely nothing to do with reality, but when you're employed in a job you're not crazy about with bosses over you who are less than respectable, reality is not exactly what you're looking for. The views of white, sandy beaches and aquamarine waters are the escape you need, and you are very vulnerable to their influence and the advertisers who shamelessly peddle them.

Take, for instance, the photos themselves. When you're shopping for a boat it's a bit akin to looking for a relationship in on online dating service. The pictures are there, and no matter how much you try to remind yourself that the pictures are of a made-up, dressed-up, and possibly photo-shopped girl, you see what you want to see. Often, the pictures aren't recent. Sometimes they're pictures of the boat from when the seller bought it, which might have been *years* ago. Sometimes the pictures are stock pictures of the model of the boat, but not that boat in particular and are marked "sister ship." Even if you *know* that up front, your mind will still associate the pristine condition of the stock picture to the boat in the ad you are looking at, and the sellers know that. If you're unsure of the time frame of the pictures, you can sometimes get the date information from the picture by right-clicking the photo and going to Properties. It doesn't always have that information, but sometimes you get lucky.

The pictures in the ad of our Tartan were beautiful. The interior was clean, cute little dinner plates set out on the table, wine bottle and wine glasses set out, pretty little throw pillows everywhere. When we went to see the actual boat it was difficult to tell it was even the same boat. The pictures were taken more than six months prior, and a lot of abuse had

The ad picture of the salon

happened in the interim. If you decide to contact an owner about a boat you see in an ad, ask when the pictures were taken. Write it down and who told you. You may need it later. These pictures of the galley are the ad picture on the left, and as we found it on the right.

The ad picture of the galley

The actual galley as we found it

As you look through the ad, remind yourself to look at the *whole* ad. A lot of people look at the pictures seeing only what they like. Look for tell-tale signs of water intrusion along the floor in the pictures. Look for signs of water intrusion along ports and hatches. Look for signs of unremediated mold. If the photographer has done his work well, these things will not be visible, but you can at least eliminate the immediately visible traumas before you waste money going to look. Look for a "staged" feel. Usually if the photos have been staged, there is something they don't want you to see.

In our case it was the missing V-berth mattress. The V-berth had been staged with blankets and pillows to look like there was one there but, alas, it ended up being a deception. We only found this out after the agreement was signed. The owners were to come to the boat and remove their personal belongings as well as to bring the few things they had at

The staged v-berth "mattress"

their house back to the boat. Whoops. No mattress. Oh, did we forget to mention that?

There are honest boat sellers out there. I know this because *we* were, but the vast majority of boat deals we encounter have taken advantage of the dreamy-eyed prospective cruiser. Enjoy pouring over all of the yachtworld.com ads with that dreamy-eyed view for a time, then pull yourself back down to Earth for the real search.

After a few months of that dreaming, I started our first spreadsheet, the first of many that we used over our 6-year journey toward casting off the dock lines. In the spreadsheet, I put all of the characteristics that we were looking for in a blue water cruiser. The spreadsheet brought me back down to Earth, and our serious boat search began. As we looked over ads and went to boat shows, we charted each prospective boat on the spreadsheet, giving them a point for every characteristic that each boat had, and tallying their total scores. I can just hear you laughing right now. Yes, we were ridiculously detailed in our search, something that will not surprise you if you happen to know any pilots personally. Here is our list of requirements. As I look this over now, I'm surprised that there is very little I would add or change in the requirements of a blue water cruiser.

Monohull Desired Characteristics

1. Modified fin keel: maneuvers better in tight spaces and points higher to windward

2. Reasonable beam (3:1 or so): makes for a more sea-kindly boat

3. Low cabin trunk: lower center of gravity for stability

4. Cockpit seats long enough to sleep on: benefits a short-handed crew

5. High bridgedeck to companionway: to prevent down-flooding into the cabin if you take a wave into the cockpit

6. Medium freeboard: balance between interior space, ease of boarding, and less spray into the cockpit in waves

7. Hatches>= 24x24: enable escape by the average-sized person in an emergency as well as adequate ventilation

8. Locking washboards: prevents washboards falling out if the boat is knocked down and the cabin flooding as a result

9. Softer bilges: more directional stability and takes chop better

10. Heavy displacement: more stable, more sea-kindly

11. Skeg hung rudder: to protect the rudder from impact damage

12. Cutter rig: to provide more possible sail configurations

13. L or U-shaped galley: better security for the cook when underway in rough seas

14. Drawers in galley: personal storage preference for utensils

15. Separate shower: so you don't have to dry the head off to use it

16. Adequate handholds: for security when moving around underway in rough seas

17. Wide companionway steps: more secure for older sailors

18. Adequate cleats: necessary for adequate dock lines

19. Metal toe rail or raised bulwarks: better for securing things like fenders, prevents tool and equipment loss over the side

20. Smaller windows: not susceptible to breakage in rough seas

21. Topping lift: for better control of the boom

22. Boom vang: for better control of the boom

23. Tracks well (little leeway): for shorter sail times on passages

24. Dual helm: easier to see to dock

25. Inboard shrouds: for good pointing

26. Engine of at least 1hp per foot of boat length for adequate power when motoring

27. Solid fiberglass hull (at least below the waterline for impact protection)

Over the course of our boat shopping we looked at hundreds of possible models but pretty quickly reduced that number down to a half dozen or so that we were really very interested in. Toward the end of our search we ended up with 5 particular individual boats that we were looking at and I've listed the scores for those five boats here. These scores are their scores out of 27 possible points. Before you wonder, the Tartan was not the highest score, but the ones with higher scores also came with higher price tags so, as with most boat-related decisions, we came to a compromise. By the time you buy a boat you will be sick of hearing the well-abused quote, "All things on a boat are a compromise." Like all things in life, though, clichés such as this are formed from the grain of truth that they reveal.

Passport 40: 24
Pacific Seacraft 40: 25
Jeanneau 42i: 17
J-40: 16
Tartan 42: 23

This spreadsheet was constructed from information we gathered from months of research. We read books, we listened to old salts and, whenever we could, we talked to cruisers. Our biggest mistake here was that we were married to the idea that we were going to be hard-core blue water cruisers. We rarely even entertained any other possibility, a situation that was largely my doing because I simply don't care for the modern sailboat style that is prevalent in coastal cruisers. Every boat we looked through at the boat shows left me cold. They were institutionally devoid of any homey feeling, and this was going to be my full-time home. My husband, on the other hand, loved the sleeker lines and the ground-up designed arches and the larger cockpits. After taking our blue water training voyages he demurred, seeing that open ocean crossings in boats with wide, open interiors is probably not the safest means of travel. But his love of the modern cruising boat never faltered and I'm grateful that he was willing to acquiesce to my needs for atmosphere. Your spreadsheet, if you're ridiculously detail-oriented like us, will need to reflect your style of cruising, so adjust it accordingly.

Once we began crystallizing our ideal boat, the search became much more focused. When we saw a boat we thought might work, we put it into the spreadsheet and tallied up the score. With our total possible score of 27, we were willing to look at any boat that had a score of 22 or more, although we did look at a few below that, more by means of comparison than anything else. Even with our narrowed search specifications, finding a boat that met both our needs and our wants was not going well. We were limited in funds as well as limited in travel time since we were both still working full-time at this point. Most of the boats that fit the bill were far away.

During this time we were also attending the boat shows. We attended the Annapolis Strictly Sail show in October three years running as well as the Chicago Strictly Sail show in January four years. Clearly all of the boats at the shows were way out of our price range, but they did give us the opportunity to get inside multiple different boats and to get a feel for the general style of the different manufacturers. It was also a good chance to view the various vendor products and get a feel for the types of equipment we wanted on the boat. Mostly, though, it was a great get-away from the severe winters of the Midwest, a way to keep the dream alive when it seemed impossible to do so. Searching for a boat can be a daunting process. It's easy to get discouraged and to let that discouragement draw you away from your dream. Dreams must be cultivated in the same way that a garden must be or they will die.

It was in the middle of one of the worst Midwest winters that we'd had in recent memory that we parked our car in the long-term parking and hopped onto an Amtrak train headed for the Strictly Sail Chicago. It was snowing, and it was good to be in the warm comfort of the train car instead of driving among the crazies on the highway for hours. We spent the trip looking at—what else—boat ads and talking about what we might see at the show. We were going early this year, taking advantage of the VIP Thursday and the lack of long lines, and planned on returning the next day before all the crowds even got there. We spent the day Thursday touring the various boats in the lineup: Hunters, Catalinas, Jeaneaus, Beneteaus, a Compac or two and some J-boats. All of them the new, sleek, all-plastic production boats. Hotel rooms. Not homes. The last boat we toured on that Thursday was the Tartan 4400. I can't remember the exact 2011 dollar amount, but it was somewhere approaching a million in cold cash. I descended the companionway steps first, and before Tim even had a chance to get from the cockpit below I turned to him and said, "If our checkbook would support the price of this boat I'd write one today." I could feel the difference in the boat immediately. The joinery was high quality, the design was warm and homey. Spaces were laid out well. The galley was a dream. It was fun, but reality was reality and we didn't have any rich uncles loitering in the wings.

That evening when we got back to the hotel, Tim was channel surfing and I was looking online at used Tartans. If we couldn't afford a new one, could we afford a used one? There, on yachtworld.com, was a 1982 Tartan 42. The boat was in Chicago and the broker was at the boat show. I turned the screen toward Tim and said, "What do you think about this one?"

The following morning we headed back to the boat show and found the broker's booth. We made arrangements to come back the following weekend to see the boat. We were cautiously optimistic as we left the boat show. Little did we know...

Notes

5 SURVEY(S), SEA TRIAL(S), AND CON MEN

Human beings are intuitive creatures. Very often we know a thing that can't be known or suspect a thing there is no reason to suspect. It's why pilots stand on the ramp looking at the sky, sailors stand on the bow feeling the motion of the sea, and mothers take a firmer grip on the little one's hand. The weekend after the Chicago Boat Show, Deb and I were back on the train, headed north to see the Tartan 42 for the first time. We were far from being committed to buying that particular boat, but we both knew a corner had been turned. Similar to when we had made the decision to buy a "starter boat" and ended up with *Nomad*, we had made the decision it was time to start looking for "the boat."

We were four years into our five year plan, and suspected there were probably three, maybe four more yet to go. The economy was struggling and, like everyone else, we had taken a beating in the housing market. Deb had run afoul of a real low-life of a boss and our combined income had taken a hit. Other financial pressures had limited the amount we could invest, so our retirement funds had yet to reach the level we thought we needed. But somehow we knew it was time to start looking.

There was a serious debate as to the general path we should take. One was to hold on to *Nomad*, move her east, live on her while we looked for right boat, trade her in, and start cruising from there. There was still some small hope that we would find a catamaran in our price range. It would have to be located somewhere we could start our cruising since shipping it anywhere was clearly out of the question. The more we thought about it the more it seemed that leaping directly onto a new boat, in a new place, to start a new kind of living was leaping into the deep end with total abandon. We are not total abandon kind of people and so considered a different approach.

After four years on *Nomad* we were not as wedded to the multi-hull idea as we had been. It would be nice, but we both knew it was a stretch. At that point it still seemed likely that we were three or four years from setting out as well. By refinancing the house we could buy a 38 to 45 foot mono-hull in reasonable shape, have it shipped to Carlyle, and get it ready to cruise while we still had income. Such a boat would fit on the lake (barely), there was a travel lift that could handle it (barely), and there was a dock at Boulder long enough to hold it (barely). At Carlyle we had the support of a sailing community we dearly loved, access to people who knew things we still had to learn, and we could sail the boat in familiar waters with friends who routinely chartered boats that size and larger. Instead of leaping into the deep end with abandon, we would wade in carefully until the water closed in over our heads.

We didn't know it at the time, but our search for "the boat" was handicapped from the very beginning. We bought *Nomad* without a survey, at the marina we ended up calling home more than six years, and through a broker who had his boat parked right next to ours. In our circle of sailing friends this was normal. Buying the first boat was scary, but went really well. We ended up selling *Nomad* for more than we paid, in a painless transaction that spoke well of all involved. We were honest about what we bought. We were honest about what we sold. We had no clue how rare that is in the retail, used-sailboat world.

A second handicap was a life-long involvement in the world of aviation, one of the most regulated industries on the planet. In that world, manufacturers get a production certificate from the Federal Aviation Administration for every type of airplane they produce. The tooling is certified. The inspection system is certified. There is a common saying that the very first rivet cannot be driven, the very first piece of metal cannot be cut, nor the very first piece of hardware sourced, until the weight of the paperwork equals that of the finished aircraft.

Once the aircraft is built and sold, only those properly certified can get behind the controls and make it go. Only those with the proper certification can perform maintenance on the engines, and only those with a different certification can do maintenance on the airframe. Quite literally, a person who is certified to change the fuel control system on a jet may not be legally qualified to drive a rivet in the wing. Often, a person with a different certification will be required to inspect the maintenance that is done. The mechanics and inspectors will describe the work done in a logbook, sign and date their entry, and include the certification number that they carry. That maintenance paperwork will follow the aircraft for its entire operating life and must be transferred when the aircraft finds a new owner. Some of that same paperwork, any that pertains to major modifications or repairs, is duplicated and stored by the FAA. A copy is available to anyone who wants one.

The parts that go on aircraft are certified, though that does not mean they are certified for any airplane. Early in my career I inspected a small, single engine airplane, that had been modified with a larger engine. Its 100hp Continental 0-200 had been replaced by a Lycoming 0-320-A1B of 150hp. The paperwork authorizing the replacement (called a Supplemental Type Certificate, or STC) did not list the -A1B as an approved model. A whole group of people found themselves in a bind: the mechanic who installed the engine, the inspector who approved the installation as being done in accordance with the STC, and the owner who paid for the whole thing and found himself with an aircraft that could not be legally flown or insured. Since he had been flying the airplane, his pilot certificate was also at risk. I know this was a big deal because I was in the hanger with the FAA inspector who started the proceedings against all involved.

The downside to all of these requirements is that airplanes are unbelievably expensive to produce, purchase, and operate. The upside is that pretty much everyone involved has at least a clue as to what they are doing. In addition, the machinery meets rigid standards and there is a running record of the maintenance that has been performed pretty much since the day the thing came out of the factory. It isn't perfect of course, but not to due to a lack of effort.

As it turns out, that is not even close to the reality of the marine world of cruising sailboats. Not knowing, we jumped into that particular deep end with both feet. We nearly drowned. Our first mistake was looking for a boat without giving much thought to the broker who came with it.

Tip → → *Trust your own instincts in every part of a boat deal.*

We had dismissed current production boats, "current" being less than 10 years old for a couple of simple reasons. First, they were way more than we could even dream of spending. The second was just as easy: Deb didn't like them. Each one we explored over several years of attending both the Chicago and Annapolis boats shows, she dismissed as too much like a hotel room. None of them felt like a "home" for her and that pretty much was the end of that.

The older production boats presented an entirely different problem. Our impression, based on hundreds of conversations with sailors of all different backgrounds and experience levels, was that those boats carried serious questions about build quality. Those built during down years in the economy, when new boat sales were very sensitive to asking price, were often mentioned as not being up to the rigors of open water sailing. Manufacturers, we were told, had cut corners to cut costs, using cheaper materials and build methods. Boats built with chopped fiberglass in the hulls were specific targets of derision, ones to be avoided if at all possible. We struggled to come up with even a general specification of age and type of boat we might consider. A visit to the Chicago Boat Show offered a path out of our wilderness.

Our annual trek to the Chicago Boat Show was our favorite trip of the year. We would ride the train from St. Louis, spend a night or two in a nice hotel for a not-completely-ludicrous price, have a nice meal, and see some nice boats. Often we would run into friends, making the whole thing just that much more fun.

In early 2011 the snow was flying and the temperatures brutally cold in Chicago, but the train didn't mind. The show hosted the normal number of boats offered by Hunter, Beneteau, Catalina, etc. All were pretty boats, all were out of our price range, and none passed Deb's "this is a home" test. There was one exception, the new Tartans. True, they were far, far, out of our price range (what we called Lottery Boats) but the rich wood interiors and solid feel had Deb feeling "right at home." That night, back at the hotel, she started an internet search for used Tartans. As it turned out there was a 1982 Tartan 42 listed, the boat on the hard in Chicago and the broker having a booth at the show. Serendipity, right?

Next morning we were back at the Tartan display once again. An off the record chat with one of the sales reps went something like this:

"I love your boats but you are way out of my league, money wise. I'm thinking of looking at an older model, say early 80s. Am I making a mistake?"

"See that boat behind you?" he asked pointing at a new Tartan 4100, *"We built that boat exactly the same way we built the older ones. And we expect that new one to last 100 years. How old are you?"*

The odds of me still being around to sail on my 126th birthday seem kind of slim. I felt better about looking at this older boat. From the Tartan booth we walked over to meet the broker, and made our first major mistake.

Not to put too fine of an edge on it, but the broker was a flake. I took an instant dislike to him. But as he represented a boat we wanted to see, it seemed silly to let a bad first impression keep us from even taking a look. Arrangements were made for us to return the following weekend and inspect the boat. Thus was made our second major mistake.

It was January in Chicago. Several feet of snow blanketed the area. The boat was shrink-wrapped and on the hard with the batteries removed. Just what was our hurry? The boat wasn't going to go anywhere. No one else was looking at it. What we should have done was spent the rest of the winter searching, thinking, and debating. If the Tartan still seemed like a viable choice, it would be there in the spring. Instead, we waded through the snow from the Metro station to the boat yard. We were walking because the broker couldn't be bothered to arrange a ride for us, which brings us back to mistake number one. If the broker can't be bothered, don't bother with the broker. For the fact is, good boat deals actually do grow on trees. If one is missed, no worries. Another will be along in a few weeks at most, and all will be well with the world.

Instead of turning straight back to the hotel, we forged on. At least a path had been dug to the boat, a ladder put up, and an extension cord run so there was light and some heat inside. Inside, the boat looked nothing like the pictures. There was trash everywhere. The sink was full of rusty coke cans. Other cans had been left in the refrigerator, and had frozen and burst in the cold. Lockers were stuffed full of junk, paperwork was scattered hither and yon, she was clearly a boat owned by someone who didn't really care much. That should have been enough to have us scurrying back to the hotel as quickly as possible.

If no one bothers to make the boat presentable, assume there are serious problems hidden underneath the trash. But what we saw under the trash was a beautiful teak interior, a reputation for a solid boat built for serious water, a modified full keel, and a skeg hung rudder. The head was forward rather than aft, which was not favorable. The galley, however, was pretty close to perfect so far as Deb was concerned. The aft cabin held promise as a place to rest grandkids when they came for a visit. The forward v-berth was huge. We looked and poked and prodded for hours, sat in the cabin and tried to find any reason that this boat would not work for us. None came to mind and we decided to try and close the deal. We should have tried harder and paid more attention to what was staring us right in the face.

I think the broker was surprised when we said we were interested. The yard owner gave us a ride back to the hotel. Once back in St. Louis we started the task of lining up the ducks. Deb did most of the work arranging the financing while I was tasked with determining the true condition of the boat, what it might need in the way of repairs, and settling on an offering price.

I had done the inspection on *Nomad*. For the next 4 years I learned about boat systems working on her. But this Tartan was a serious piece of kit. More importantly, we were basically putting everything we had into making a cruising life. The boat would be the foundation of that life. My years in aviation had taught me that one goes to an expert to get an expert job done. I did not consider myself an expert in the marine world, and so made mistakes three through eight.

3.   Hiring a surveyor and trusting his work.

4.   Hiring both rigging and mechanical inspectors from the yard, and trusting their work.

5. Contracting with the yard to do some of the repair needed and trusting that work.

6. Deciding that having three different inspections done on the boat could stand in for sea trials.

7. Paying way too much for the boat based on the surveyor and inspector reports.

8. Not going back to Chicago, beating the broker senseless, then burning the boatyard to the ground when it all fell apart. (OK just kidding on that one.)

There are competent, careful, professional surveyors in the marine world. And it's true. It only took us eight years and four tries to find one. (So far as we can tell very few other cruisers have found a good one either.) We had a list of surveyors working in the Chicago area. I talked with several and hired a retired Navy Submarine Commander with a Master's degree in engineering.

The majority of the maintenance technicians in the marine world are competent, careful, and professional. Or so I have been told. And, the fact is, I have met one or two of them in my travels. Well, maybe three. They are the exception. The two hired to look at the Tartan, and the surveyor, were given the same instructions. They were being paid, by me, to find everything they could find wrong with the boat. This was a pre-buy inspection and, as such, should go well beyond anything that could be described as a routine look. Throw every switch, work every system, look in every dark hole, anything that looks wrong or catches the eye? Figure out why, and then we will figure out what needs to be fixed.

I am convinced they never even got on the boat. The most serious item on the survey was that the wood on the helm was rough and needed refinished. The only notable discrepancies of the rigging and maintenance inspection were a gray water pump didn't work, and a crack in the spreader bracket on the mast. The pump I wasn't too worried about, and I contracted with the yard to get the mast welded. The yard, by the way, is one of the largest and best known in the Chicago area. Real experts, or so I was told.

Based on the survey and inspections, a price was agreed to and the deal struck. A separate contract was made with the yard to have the boat prepped for shipping and put on a truck. This turned out to be the only thing they managed to do without any obvious screw-up.

TJ

The trucking company we used turned out to be the best part of the experience. Several months after seeing the Tartan in the snow the truck pulled into Tradewinds Marina on Lake Carlyle. It was the same marina where the first sailing class had launched this adventure. It was also the only marina on the lake with a travel lift big enough to handle the boat.

I am not a big one for talismans or superstitions. But when the travel lift ran out of gas, leaving us swinging several feet above the water, maybe I should have started to wonder. We hung there for more than an hour while they figured out how to climb up to the tank to add some fuel. When the lift was coaxed back to life it turned out the lake level was so low that the keel sunk down into the mud as the straps fell away. A friend and his powerboat were needed to drag us out of the lift pit. When he then had to pull the bow around to get us pointed toward the lake I really should have started to suspect that all was not well with our world.

The mast had been dropped at our home marina to be stepped later, so our first trip in the Tartan was a motor across the lake. It went pretty well though, as it turned out, we were eating up much of the engine time we had left to play with.

Notes

6 WHEN TO WALK AWAY
(A waterspout? Really?)

I was a bit surprised to find a hold-harmless agreement in the paperwork for that first survey. That turns out to be a standard in the marine industry and is still a puzzle to me. In the aviation world one will be held directly responsible if an inspection misses some impending failure, particularly if that failure ends up in loss of life or limb. But a marine surveyor, it turns out, has no such concern. Before any of them will look at a boat the owner will sign a piece of paper that states the surveyor cannot be held liable for anything missed. If, for example, the boat goes directly from the hard after a survey, gets set into the water, and sinks straight to the bottom because the keel feel off, the water poured in, none of the pumps worked, and it wouldn't have mattered if they did work because all of the hoses had rotted off and the through hulls were glassed over, the surveyor doesn't get any of the blame or take any responsibility. A survey is done by a person who has absolutely no skin in the game.

He has his money. I promise he has his money because no one gets a copy of the survey until he does. Until the insurance company gets a copy of that survey, the boat will not be insured. Until the boat is insured it isn't likely the yard is going to put it in their lift, nor would any owner want it to. Boats have been known to fall out of lifts and most yards are counting on the boat's insurance to pick up the tab if it does. And therein lies the scam. The survey is required by the insurance company, but the surveyor has no liability. Which would not seem to matter because the insurance company knows it is a useless bit of paper anyway. Let me say that again, the insurance companies are well aware that the survey is a joke.

Perhaps that is a bit of an overstatement. More accurately *my* insurance company knows the survey is a joke. I know that because they told me so. They told me so as a result of a second survey we had done on the Tartan just before we shipped it east to go cruising. During the intervening couple of years we had done a ton of work, installed some systems, and generally added significantly to the value of the boat. Before it went into a travel lift and onto a truck for a nearly 800 mile journey, we wanted the hull value raised. To get that increase we had to have a second survey done. It turned out to be worse than the first.

The first survey missed virtually everything that was wrong with the boat, but the second surveyor invented things that were NOT wrong with the boat. My favorite was "universal hydraulic migration," apparently survey-speak for hull blistering. Hull blistering may or may not be a real thing in the marine world. I am not going to get into that debate. But what I do know is that it wasn't a real thing on our Tartan. In this case "universal hydraulic migration" was repaired by sanding off most of the 15 or so coats of old bottom paint, thus removing 99.9 % of the "blisters." Putting on four fresh coats of bottom paint finished the "repair" of the "universal hydraulic migration." The very few real blisters found barely penetrated the gel coat and were easily fixed with a bit of grinding and a some thickened resin.

It was also reported that we had "hull flexing" around the propeller shaft strut. This area of the hull is solid fiberglass shaped in a "V." It was like claiming a beer bottle was flexing. What he was seeing was deteriorated fairing compound, stuff universally known as "bondo." Bondo is not nearly as tough as fiberglass, and will eventually succumb to being soaked in water. It is used throughout the marine industry to make hulls smooth and pretty. (Don't take that as some kind of criticism. It is used throughout the aviation industry for the exact same reason). The bondo on any older hull is going to need repaired. It has nothing to do with structure, and is an easy fix. Any shop class kid can probably do a pretty good job (but don't let him play with fiberglass repairs).

Tip →→ *Track down and talk to as many of the previous owners that you can before committing to purchase.*

These, and a few other pure make-believe items, were noted in his "survey." Since I had learned my lesson the first time around and was standing right by the side of the second surveyor, I knew it was make-believe. I pointed out to him that it was make-believe. Didn't matter, it went in the report anyway. So I ended up explaining to the insurance company that it was make-believe. They told me they knew that already. Really? Then what, prey tell, is the purpose for this entire charade? I was never told, but had to pay the surveyor anyway.

As it turns out, what the first survey on our boat really, really missed, was that it had been hit by a waterspout. That hit tore the bow pulpit clean off the boat, taking the anchor as well as stripping out all of the anchor chain. The roller furler and stay were ripped off and had to be replaced as well as all of the anchor fittings and windlass mount. Both toe rails were damaged and, apparently, the boat got shoved backwards into shallow water. Both the skeg and the rudder were damaged. None of this, by the way, was mentioned by either surveyor.

We did not find out about this little incident until the boat had been shipped east and was undergoing final preparations to go cruising. Over the months we had been working toward this point we had tracked down as many of the previous owners as we could. One had some paperwork lying around and agreed to mail it to us. Buried in the middle of that packet was the work order detailing the damage and the repairs. A work order we had missed in the crunch of the never ending to-do list needing to be completed before we could set out. Given the damage listed, the boat should have been totaled. Given the cost of the repairs listed, it was clear that the repairs had been done on the cheap and the boat put out on the market. In other words, the owner before us bought a totaled boat, sold us a totaled boat, and we have been fixing it ever since.

In hindsight, there were so many indications that this was a boat that we should have walked away from, and we missed them all. Before I review the thickness of my skull, let me say this. I know sailors like to give their hearts to a boat. Trust me, the boats do not love us back. A boat is a collection of fiberglass, wood and metal. It is wires and hoses, pistons and pumps. Maybe, after we have been with one for a while, it will share a bit of our soul. But it will not come with one of its own. The only rational way to approach buying a boat is with a mindset that, if a boat really is necessary (and if the plan is to go cruising, a boat is certainly necessary) any particular boat is one that should not be bought. That's right, look at any boat as one that should be walked away from, and then try to find reasons not to do so.

One look at our broker and we should have smiled and walked away. Actually, we should have run screaming for the nearest exit. Why buy a boat from a loon? This is a big deal. Look for some kind of professionalism, an effort to appear competent even if that is an illusion. This person needs to do the best possible job that can be done just to offer a fighting chance that the new owner of an older boat will not get completely slammed. Find a broker that gives off waves of warm and fuzzies, who can't do enough, who has a clean shirt with a collar and maybe even a tie. Find one who can afford to rent a nice office, who has hot coffee or a cold drink to offer from a nice looking and clean kitchenette. Let him or her help in finding the right boat, but make them earn their commission. A good broker's commission is the best money spent in any boat deal.

Even with the help of a good broker, never forget that any particular boat is one that can, and probably should, be walked away from. Until the broker is utterly convincing that any particular boat is worth a serious look, don't bother.

It is likely the broker will soon get a lead on the "right" boat. When that happens take a hard, serious, look. Get a head full of wonderful images, of anchoring off a white sand beach or romping across a sparkling sea on a screaming close reach. Sit in the cockpit and imagine sundowners and sun sets. Smile, nod, dream...and walk away.

Yep, walk away from that first real prospect. Shed a tear if necessary, but walk away. It is good practice. It will set the proper tone for the head, harden the heart, and give the broker a chance to earn his or her cut. Look at some other boats. I'm not saying that first boat can't be the boat in a week or a month. In all likelihood it will still be around. And if not, remember what I said earlier. Good boat deals do, in fact, grow on trees. Another will be along shortly. It the broker is any good, he or she will know about it.

Once a real deal is in the works, never be committed to seeing it through. Try to find a surveyor who is worth the money, but do not worry much if that does not seem possible. Just make sure he understands that, on the day of the survey, he is not going to be alone. You are going to be there. The broker should be there as well. Bring along a friend who knows something about boats. Or bring along a friend who knows about cars or airplanes or motorcycles and likes to ask questions. Hell, bring along a friend who doesn't know anything but knows how to fake it. If the surveyor has a problem with any of this, get a different one.

Useless as they may be, if the survey turns up anything that looks the least bit odd, call it a day and walk away. It might be evidence of a lightning hit, water stains where there shouldn't be water stains, oil in the bilge, a missing this or that, doesn't matter. Also, give the surveyor a copy of the listing for the boat. Many listings include a list of equipment. A specific instruction to any surveyor must be that every single item on that equipment list is actually on the boat and functioning properly in every single mode it has. Any that do not function perfectly should be stricken from the list and the price adjusted accordingly. The thing might be repairable but, particularly if it is an older system on an older boat, replacing it will likely be the only option.

A good example from our Tartan was the autopilot. We were assured that it was inspected, checked, and functioned properly. It wasn't and it didn't. The manufacturer was years out of business and no parts were available to even attempt a repair. Five thousand dollars and many hours of labor later, we sail open water with a Cape Horn wind vane. No boat is perfect, but don't let that be an excuse for buying one that should have been left alone.

58

Get a list of every previous owner and make a timeline that covers the years from the day the boat went to its first owner until the day you are standing, looking at the thing. Any gaps? Walk away. Talk to the previous owners if possible. I will never buy another boat that I can't talk to everyone who owned it before me. Even though no official record of its history is required by the marine industry, doesn't mean a near equivalent cannot be put together by a careful buyer.

If the previous owner comes across as "wrong" in any way, walk away. Listen to the sub-conscious, it will often make correct calls for reasons the thinking mind didn't notice. And I mean little things: a fleeting look of guilt across a face, the inability to look someone in the eye, some hedging over this issue or that. An email that never gets answered or a phone call that never gets returned? Head straight for the door. There is absolutely no reason that this particular deal needs to happen. In all likelihood no one needs this person's boat nearly as bad as he or she needs to be rid of it.

If, after all this, the deal is still alive, make an honest offer. Don't even think of trying to get a "steal." Maybe, somewhere, someone gets one of those once in a while. But I kind of doubt it. If it is a "steal" someone wants it gone. Don't be the fool that steals it. On the other hand, if the owner can't be budged off a price that seems too high, walk away. Consider all deals dead deals until the money changes hands. Then go celebrate doing the best job that could be done in finding the "right boat."

Notes

7 MAINTENANCE IN PARADISE

Even if one buys a brand new, fresh-off-the-boat-show-dock cruising boat, maintenance in paradise will be part of the life. From some of the stories we have heard, such a purchase is fraught with its own potentials for clashes over who is going to pay for what, warranties notwithstanding. Those of us living in the world of a used boat being the ticket to paradise, have different concerns: buying the soundest, best-maintained cruising boat we can find at a reasonable price, and keeping it working once we leave to go cruising.

Avoiding Maintenance in Paradise

My dad was a mechanical engineer with a focus on the effects of vibration and sound on complex systems: systems like nuclear submarines and nuclear power plants, and vibrations like those that come with earthquakes and anti-submarine ordinance. After he retired, he helped me design and get Federal Aviation Approval for a vibration analysis program that extended the overhaul requirements on a fleet of turbine engines from 6000 hours of operating time to "on condition."

I spent a lifetime in the aviation maintenance world. My next youngest brother went to commercial diving school, spent a couple of decades fixing mining equipment deep underground rather than deep underwater, and then moved on to working with some of the largest mobile cranes in the world. He is, in my opinion, a mechanic without peer, one of the best maintenance technicians I have ever seen pick up a wrench. To this day, I wish my hands had half the talent of his. My youngest brother went into the auto repair business. He is a true Mr. Goodwrench. Not the kind that gets on TV in a tidy uniform, clean rag in hand, waving a shiny socket wrench at the camera. He is the one car owners really, really hope is the guy fixing their ride. In my life nearly everyone is a mechanic to some degree, and most are pros working in tough, regulated environments. My view of doing maintenance in paradise is heavily skewed toward those having at least some of the skills needed.

This, I think, is an important consideration. One of the goals of cruising is to live a different way than one did on land. More mobile, less dependent on complex infrastructure, taking on most of the responsibility for one's own well being. It is amazing how little water it takes, lying between a boat and shore, for that level of responsibility to rise dramatically. Just a couple of hundred feet away from land and any repair becomes a matter of doing it with the tools and parts on board, with only the skill in the skipper's hands. Help, additional parts, and special tools are all likely a dink launch and ride, then a long walk away. This is a "do it yourself" kind of lifestyle.

Our experience with doing maintenance in paradise started long before paradise ever broached the horizon. As mentioned earlier, our starter boat, *Nomad*, was a well-maintained little thing by marine standards. But here is where an ugly truth rears its head. "Do it yourself" is a world completely devoid of standards. What one might consider "more than good enough" another will find to be an embarrassing hack job, one that can't be tolerated for another moment. There is considerable room for interpretation. We had *Kintala* shipped to a yard on the Chesapeake to start our cruising life, and needed to do a lot of final prep to get going. The good folks at Oak Harbor Marina encouraged owners to do their own work, often loaning tools and offering good advice. One of their lead technicians, upon learning I was an aircraft mechanic, made the following observation, *"You airplane guys always do a job ten times better than it needs to be done, spending ten times the money and time."*

In a perfect world all mechanical devices would also be perfect. In *this* world a mechanical device is close enough to being perfect if it is working reliably and doesn't look too butchered up. In cases where a failure would put people at risk, some kind of alternate or back up system is sometimes considered an adequate level of safety. Sometimes. In any case, it doesn't have to be perfect, it just has to work.

I have another balance for my inner perfectionist, taught me by my grandfather, a life-long professional truck mechanic. *"Getting it perfect,"* he taught me at a very young age, *"will always keep you from getting it done."*

For all of that, my experience with the marine industry is that getting it to work at all is sometimes near a miracle, getting it to work reliably sometimes near impossible. No one ever, ever, gets even the smallest job "perfect."

There will be times when getting something working will simply be beyond the reach of the skills, tools, and parts on board. When that happens, doing without until the boat is in a different place where repairs can be accomplished becomes the key to success. Here is where a second ugly truth rears its head.

Boats break. Boats break a lot. In fact, it could be said that every boat, everywhere, is broken all the time. They are just waiting for the most inopportune moment to inform the crew of what isn't working. The cruising life is a life where fixing the boat is as much a part of the deal as anchoring off white sand beaches and sailing deep blue water. The idea behind buying a good cruising boat is to get one where these required repairs do not become the ONLY part of a cruising life.

For the most part, houses don't leak. Cars don't leak. Airplanes don't leak much either. But boats built to operate in a water environment? They leak like "secrets" from a Senate sub-committee. All the time, everywhere, and particularly when no one is really paying much attention. When it comes to leaks, the kind sailors worry most about are those where the water the boat is floating in gets into the boat instead. This is, of course, a good way to ruin an otherwise nice day. But when it comes to buying a boat, this kind of leak isn't the one at the top of the list of leaks to address first. First on the list should be deck leaks.

Fiberglass boats might be better thought of as cheap, plywood boats with a layer of fiberglass wrapped around inside and out. More expensive ones might have end grain balsa wood wrapped instead. In either case, any of that wood that has been exposed to water is starting to rot. Any older boat that has had hardware added or replaced on the deck, or seen any kind of damage repaired, has water leaking into that core. My point being that any older cruiser boat most likely has rotten spots in the deck and / or hull. The broker, and most likely the surveyor, will not talk of rotten spots. That place on the deck isn't "rotten", it's "soft". The impression is that a little light labor will make it all good. Don't pay attention to the boat-speak: think "rotten." A badly rotted boat is a bad boat, one to be avoided at all costs.

It isn't that a boat with any rotten spots will be unsafe. It isn't that such a boat will sink as soon as the first wave washes over it. But, sooner rather than later, the rotten parts of the deck will have to be repaired. Such a task is neither easy nor cheap, and the costs go up exponentially with the size of the area needing repaired. Even worse, getting a quality deck repair done is by no means a sure thing regardless of the money spent.

On the very first visit to a potential boat, assuming the initial look-see didn't provoke a "walk-away" response, the next item should be a slow walk about of the deck. Take off the shoes, go slow and easy, listen and feel. Tread heavily on the side decks, picture stomping forward on a dark and stormy night to reset a dragging anchor. Take a stroll along the cabin top and imagine digging in to wrestle a reef into a mainsail as the winds ramp up into the "scaring silly" range. Does the deck creak like old bones in the morning? Are there crackling noises coming from underfoot? Does it feel spongy and, if so, how much and where? Big rotten spots out by the edge, where the deck and the hull join, are bad,

bad news. So are big rotten spots around a deck stepped mast. (Run brothers and sisters, run far, far away.) Smaller rotten spots near items like cleats or deck fittings are, oddly, less so. Such places are likely isolated and, perhaps, more reasonably repairable. But they will need repaired and the cost should come out of the current owner's pocket.

If the walk-about doesn't provoke thoughts of falling through the deck, make sure the survey includes a moisture check more high tech than thumping on the deck with a hammer. Yes, thumping on the deck with a soft faced hammer works. Doing one independently of any survey and then comparing findings is a good idea. But the high tech equipment isn't that expensive and the survey should include a detailed examination of both hull and deck. The importance of a sound deck and hull cannot be overstated. A boat that does not feel and sound solid, is not solid enough to buy.

Sometimes leaks in the core allow water to go all the way through to the interior. Leaks around portholes and hatches often fit this description. More times than not, when I have removed portholes for re-bedding, the core around the hole is compromised – read that as rotted to damp, ugly, smelly black chunks of gross. My fix is to dig out the rotted core and then fill the void with thickened fiberglass resin. Mounting holes will have to be drilled, and the core repair will add several hours to finishing the leak repair.

Here is a good place to make a point. Re-bedding a single port that needs some core work will take a single technician at least a full shop day to do correctly. At $50 per hour that is $450 to fix a single leak, not including materials and taxes. My current boat has twelve ports and four hatches. The last port we fixed took two full days of work. Worst case, assuming each port is a day and the hatches two days each, rebedding the average amount of ports and hatches on a 40-foot boat can lighten someone's wallet to the tune of EIGHT THOUSAND dollars, plus materials and taxes.

Think positive, and assume that an older boat that has seen at least some competent maintenance will only need half of those ports and hatches resealed in the year or so after it changes hands. Now the new owner is only out four thousand dollars to keep the inside of his or her new home dry.

Then come those really bad leaks that let big water into the boat. Thru-hull failures are the ones everyone thinks about, but are not the ones that seem to sink most boats. The real sinkers are the hoses attached to the thru-hulls. Hoses that go years without a single hand being laid upon them. Some that go years without even so much as a look. Hoses that a do-it-yourself type might have taken off then put back on with old, inferior clamps, maybe forgetting one or two. Clamps that are, sometimes, nearly impossible to see let alone reach with a wrench or screwdriver. Checking each and every one of them will require some serious effort on the part of the surveyor. The same surveyor who has no skin in the game, and isn't likely keen on leaving any skin deep in some dark recess of the boat.

Should any kind of leak disqualify any boat? No. If it worked that way the resale boat market would disappear overnight. Our boat has at least two leaks at the moment. One is a port that started leaking after our last pounding in open water. The second has defied capture so far, but it leaves a trail down the port sidewall teak. Leaks are just one of those things that seem to come with sailboats. The trick is to start out with as few as possible and then work constantly to keep them under control.

That being said, at some point before the deal is sealed the boat should have its bilge completely dried and then it should be dumped in the water, assuming it isn't already. All thru-hulls should be closed and any system that makes water which ends up in the bilge, refrigerators, air conditioners, etc., should be turned off. Go away. Have a nice dinner. Take in a movie. Go back in the morning and take a look. If the bilge is not completely dry—and I mean bone, dust, and desert dry—find out why. No deal until the leak is found, explained, and fixed as perfectly as it can be. This is especially important if the boat has a bolt-on keel.

If the boat has a bolted-on keel, and chances are it does, there can be no question of any leaks around the bolts, loose or corroded bolts, soft hull, or deteriorating bedding. None. A keel failure is a killer, pure and simple. Any indication of water coming into the hull though the keel joint should kill a boat deal dead.

Step to the very back of the boat and look forward. On any boat more than a couple of decades old it is safe to assume that nearly every single item that is bolted to the deck and cabin top, every stanchion, every port, every block and rail, bow and stern pulpit, is going to need removed and resealed in the next couple of years. Most will require at least some core repair. Not all at once, hopefully, but nearly all in any case. It will be a huge amount of work. Do it yourself or pay to get it done, either way it cannot be avoided.

It should go without saying that any system installed on the boat should be working before any money changes hands. I'm going to say it anyway because that never seems to be the case. Used boats listed for sale are relentlessly misrepresented, and the deal is often closed on a boat with known discrepancies. A broken boat should take a serious hit in its sale price. Better yet, it should be fixed before the deal is completed. The very act of fixing the broken things will undoubtedly uncover other broken things. Might as well add them to the items needing addressed before money changes hands.

Some items should just be calendar items so far as a buyer is concerned. Running rigging more than five years old? Standing rigging more than ten? Extra scrutiny is the wise person's response. Unless the rig is sitting on a stand someone gets to go up the mast and along the stays to look at every inch of it. A good trick on the standing rigging is to drag a rag along the wires. If the rag gets snagged even a single time, all the rigging needs to go away. (Our insurance company treats standing rigging as a calendar item. Since the Tartan's was more than fifteen years old, they required we replace it before taking to open water.)

Tip →→   *Talk to your insurance agent about their standing rigging age limits. Many insurance companies will not insure a boat with standing rigging older than 10 years.*

The same goes for wire lifelines. Any plastic coated wire lifelines simply have to be deposited in the nearest dumpster. In my opinion all lifelines should just go into the nearest dumpster, along with the stanchions that hold them up. Lifelines are ugly and dangerous, mostly providing assurance that, if one does fall overboard, one will hit the water head first. Take a good look at stanchions and see solid metal spikes bolted to the deck and waiting to skewer a body falling hard against them. They also provide a multitude of places for water to leak through the deck and into the interior of the boat and core.

Boats should be designed with jack lines, anchored solid, and running down the center of the deck from cockpit, to base of the mast, to fore deck. That way anyone leaving the cockpit at night or in open water can be harnessed in such a way that falling overboard is simply not possible, and without worrying about taking a solid metal rod through the heart should they fall.

Alas, mine is a minority opinion in the industry, with the Coast Guard, and with the Admiral. The best I could do was to replace our wire lines with Amsteel. Doing so cost a few hundred bucks in materials and, given my modest line splicing skills, took a couple of days. At least I know I can pull on them without them parting and leaving an open path to the open sea.

Even if visual and rag inspections come in clean, running rigging that is five years old and standing rigging more than ten, are deep into their respective service lives. The offered price should reflect the maintenance cost that is likely right around the boat life corner. This is a place of no compromise. Sailboats can live with a lot of systems problems. Smaller leaks to the core or interior will take a long time before turning into serious, boat threatening problems. But if the rig comes down all bets are off.

What to do with engines on an older boat is a special can of its own breed of worms. Small diesel engines are about the toughest little motors humankind has ever managed to produce. Pretty much any kind of maintenance will ensure they run an impressively long time, racking up thousands upon thousands of hours on the engine meter. How many hours are too many? That is the question that truly has no answer, as it depends on so much information that is simply unavailable to the prospective buyer.

One kind of engine I would avoid at all costs though, is one that has been "overhauled" in place. Likely that was done by a mechanic who is best described as a general practitioner, and he was doing a repair, not an overhaul. An engine overhaul is a major undertaking, one that needs to be done right, and one that probably should be done in a shop. The only way I would buy such a boat is if the price was reduced to the point where the engine could be replaced with the dollars saved. If the current owner is okay with cutting the price, in all likelihood he is fully aware that the engine is toast. What else did he know about that wasn't mentioned?

A quality overhaul is more likely done at a facility specializing in such work, meaning the engine was removed, shipped, repaired and re-installed. That is a major undertaking and I am doubtful such an effort makes sense unless a new engine is installed. Like most things, engine technology has changed drastically in the last few decades. Going to the bother of pulling an engine only to put an old-tech chunk of iron back in seems an opportunity lost. However, a re-powered boat comes with its own concerns.

Such a boat can be a good buy, particularly if the re-powering was done a couple of seasons ago and all of the bugs have been worked out. I would be very slow to buy a boat that has just been re-powered. Likely the current owner is going to try to get the cost of that work out of the buyer's pocket, and it isn't worth that much. Also, putting a new engine in an old boat is a huge undertaking.

Remember the story about the replaced airplane engine? There is no certification process for putting a new engine in an old boat. Engine mounts may need moved and rebuilt, meaning serious fiberglass work. Exhaust and cooling systems may need fit and re-routed, old wiring would be replaced with new. The scope of work done in fitting a new diesel in an older hull is impressive, and the opportunities for mistakes, many. Without some kind of warranty, some recourse to get things fixed, installing a new engine in an old hull may turn out to be prohibitively expensive, and the risk simply isn't worth taking. Twice in the first year of our cruising, we ran across boats that were limping back to a shop to get newly installed engines repaired. One was a catamaran that was going to need both engines removed and replaced, again. The owners were not happy sailors.

The engine in our boat is original and has been UN-affectionately dubbed the WesterBeast. It is the focus of many of the maintenance in paradise efforts. So far it has taken new engine mounts, a new injection pump, and an overhauled heat exchanger unit, to keep it grumbling away. I cringe every time the starter is engaged and all I know for sure is that it will surely cause me more grief in the future. My dream is to have it replaced with a modern engine, installed by a quality shop that is a service center for the engine manufacturer. It's a good dream. If the Beast ever rolls over and dies completely, it's a dream I will have to try and make come true.

But the true nightmare in our drive train came from the v-drive going off like a hand grenade and taking the transmission with it. This happened within ten operating hours from when we bought the boat. It was also ten operating hours from when a contracted mechanical inspection stated that the engine and drive train were in good mechanical and operating condition, and gave evidence of being well maintained. Which brings me to the one test that should be done to any prospective boat with an engine of any age.

Tip →→ *Insist on sending engine and transmission oil samples out for analysis, even if you have to pay extra for the privilege.*

Any component that has oil that gets changed as a maintenance item —engines, generators, transmissions, v-drives—should have a sample of that oil sent in for analysis. The costs are modest, the delay worth taking, and the information that analysis provides is invaluable. Until and unless those come back completely "clean" any boat deal is, at best, on life support. If there is any hesitancy on the part of anyone involved in getting the analysis done, the deal should die an instant death. If any of those tests come back indicating a potential problem, some serious negotiating and thoughts of potential, nightmare scenarios, must be handled before the deal is closed. And if the deal is closed, the one who should have taken the real beating is, in this case, the seller.

Had I been smart enough to have them done on the Tartan, the imminent failure of the v-drive could not have been missed. What was supposed to be 30 weight motor oil in the drive was, in fact, 90 weight gear oil. It is a common trick to cover up an impending gear set failure. Even the 90 weight gear oil wasn't 90 weight any more. So saturated was it with metal grindings the oil was more like paste. When I rubbed some between my thumb and finger it literally left splinters in my skin. It took nine months of frustrating effort to source and install all the items damaged when the drive broke apart. The story of that nightmare repair, conversations with the yard in Chicago, drive, transmission, and engine service representatives, and even the original designers of the boat, would make for a book all of its own. Reliving those months to write such a book though, would likely give me a stroke. It is fair to say that my entire view of the boating industry has been forever dimmed by those months.

Once the deal is closed, all further maintenance problems are in the possession of the new owner. There is no recourse if the boat turns out to be a lemon. (In my humble opinion pretty much every boat in the used cruiser fleet should be painted bright yellow, just as a reminder.) We seriously considered suing the broker, surveyor, and yard after taking possession of our current boat, but a lawyer friend suggested it would be nothing but a money maker for him. Instead, we took the dollars and buckled down to making the boat what we needed. It took nearly four years, isn't done yet, and cost nearly as much as we had spent to buy the boat in the first place.

Unavoidable Maintenance in Paradise

No matter how careful the buyer might be, how knowledgeable, how skilled, any new-to-the-buyer boat is going to need some work. Figure a third of the purchase price will be spent again within a year of buying the thing. We spent roughly $62,500 for our current boat. Before it hit cruising waters we spent at least half that much again, and we did all the labor.

A quick list of some of what we have done: new transmission, new v-drive, six new engine mounts, new prop and prop shaft, all new standing rigging, all new running rigging, all new water lines, exhaust can repair, new batteries and a repaired battery box, new head and all new hoses, new floor under the head, new pump-out deck fitting, all interior light fixtures, some new wiring, battery monitor, wind vane (in place of the non-functioning autopilot), rudder repair, skeg repair, hull repair at keel joint, rudder bearing and shoe repair, new steering cables and chain, helm lock...and that was just some of the stuff needed before this "perfectly seaworthy boat" described by the survey could be safely taken off shore.

Admittedly we got had, burned, taken to the cleaners, smacked around in a dark ally. As far as the broker, surveyor, and boat yard were concerned, the Turnip Truck *did* just drive by, hit a bump, and pitch me into their welcoming claws. And I am a world class cynic and life-long professional mechanic. The main reason for this book is to give other potential cruisers a fighting chance of finding an easier path. Going cruising is a difficult thing to pull off; many try and never actually make it. The odds are much improved if the boat isn't a huge anchor dragging one into the financial abyss.

One might wonder, had we spent $137,000 in the first place and bought a different boat, if we might have just stepped aboard and sailed happily away. Surely that seems a logical conclusion, particularly if we had enjoyed the services of reputable marine professionals. I can't say with absolute certainty such would have been the case, but stories shared with others in the cruising community suggest it's unlikely. Virtually everyone we know, who has bought and gone cruising in an older sailboat, has endured similar challenges with fitting out and getting gone. Most were not quite as bad as our experience, since I do believe (hope) that our broker, etc., were of a unique class of sleaze. But no one seems to get off easy, and a few have taken an even worse beating than we have. Anyone who has managed to toss the dock lines and gone cruising on an older sailboat should be regarded with a bit of awe. They have overcome obstacles most people cannot even imagine.

After purchase and initial repair costs, a good figure is 10% of that combined price being required per year. That 10% includes labor, so anything that can be done "in house" will go a long way toward stretching the cruising kitty. That 10% is also non-negotiable. Cruising is, in many ways, a hard life lived in a harsh environment. Salt water, waves and wind, constant use, and an occasional touch when the water is thinner than expected (which happens to everyone eventually) will keep the "to-do" list filled.

Right now we do all the maintenance on our boat ourselves but, the truth is, that will not always be the case. Maintenance is manual labor. Skilled manual labor (hopefully) but manual nonetheless. Fingers have to bend and grasp, joints have to move, the back needs to carry the load of odd positions, and eyes have to see clear enough to spot small parts in dark places. Working on boats is tough work, and a sixty year old body is not as tough as a twenty year old body. But there is a thing even those with modest or deteriorating skills can do to keep the maintenance in paradise burden bearable, and its name is "Routine." The trick to keeping any machine operating is routine, preventive maintenance, and inspection. That can sound pretty involved but, in actuality, is based on three basic ideas. Keep it clean. Work it regularly. Fix the small things.

A clean boat is a happy boat, sailed by a happy crew. When it rains, grab a deck brush and wash away the salt. On deck, polish everything that can be polished, and wax everything else. Look at it closely while polishing or waxing. I found a small crack in the bow pulpit while rubbing off the dull. We have not been near a welder since it was spotted, but I know it is there and keep an eye out for it growing into a problem. Follow rust stains on stanchions to loose screws, and replace them with new screws or blind rivets that neither rust nor loosen.

Down below a clean interior makes leaks much easier to spot. It may be awhile before they are fixed, but keeping an eye on them seems to help keep them from growing ever bigger. Replacing small pieces of rotting wood is easier than replacing big pieces of rotting wood. Always be curious, try to understand the "why" for anything out of the ordinary that is seen.

Engines, engine rooms, and bilges should be particularly clean. Any oil leaks need to be seen and known. Again, it may be awhile before they are fixed. Serious engine work at anchor or on a rolly mooring ball will make for a bitch of a day. Small issues that are known can be addressed during the next dock stop. Knowledge is the key. Sneak attacks happen only when someone doesn't know what's up.

Keep metal stuff lubed up. Things like engine mounts, throttle and shifter linkages, and hinges all benefit from a light coat of nearly any kind of thin, clean oil. Look around. I once spotted a bolt lying under the engine. Not unusual, I have found all kinds of junk lying around the machine spaces of this boat. But this bolt wasn't there the last time I looked, and it turned out to be one of those that held the valve cover in place. Sure, I know what a valve cover is, but in this case a stray bolt and an obviously empty hole where there wasn't one before was all I needed to know to keep the oil leak in check.

Hoses, belts, oil level, coolant level, hanging wires, and v-drive-to-driveshaft coupler—never start an engine until those things are checked. Anyone smart enough to make a sailboat go is smart enough to learn how do these basic "engine checks." Is the motor using oil or coolant it didn't use before? Are the belts leaving marks on the case they didn't leave before? Is anything loose or hanging that wasn't loose or hanging before? Early fixes are always easier and cheaper than late fixes, regardless of doing the work or hiring it out.

I try to take a slow walk around the deck every single day. No checklist, just a look. Do it every day and a mental picture gets etched into the sub-conscious. If something changes that makes the picture look different, that same sub-conscious will make a note and start complaining. Something as simple as a cotter key bent out of shape by snagging a jib sheet will be enough to set off the alarms. Lines chafing or sagging, an anchor chain laying odd over the bow because the snubber is fouled, a deck fitting that didn't get tightened last time around; all easy fixes as long as they are known.

Kintala normally lists to starboard because all my tools are on that side of the boat. We carry so many tools and spares on board that the quarter berth in the aft cabin was converted to a workshop / spare part storage area to hold them all. I freely admit that it's likely far more than necessary to keep a cruise underway. Still, there are some tools that every boat should carry. Keep in mind that any boat, particularly the plastic ones most of us can afford, are not really rigid. They flex, twist, and bend constantly. In addition, diesel engines and generators, by the very nature of their compression-ignition operations, shake. As a result, nearly any bolt, screw, and nut on board will eventually loosen, as if by magic. Avoiding an expensive repair is often as simple as keeping things tight.

There should be enough screwdrivers, wrenches, and sockets stashed away to reach and tighten pretty much any fastener holding things together. Of particular interest are those used to tighten up stuffing boxes. So important is the stuffing box in keeping water out of the boat that one set of wrenches should be set aside for that purpose only, marked and stored for instant and easy access.

No matter how little skill any cruiser might have when it comes to mechanical things, keeping it clean, keeping it lubed, and keeping it tight are unavoidable responsibilities. After that, the ratio of work done to work contracted out is completely up to the individual cruiser. How much does one want to do, how much can one do, and how much one trusts those being paid, will all become part of a very personal equation that is each individual cruising experience.

8 PART AND PARCEL
(Is That Piece of Equipment Really Necessary?)

One of the largest considerations when looking for your perfect cruising boat is what type of equipment is already installed on board and what you will have left to install. The list must be divided into Must Have, Probably Ought to Have, and Wish List. Set yourself up a spreadsheet or a list in a notebook and match it up against each boat you look at. Here's an example of the list. I'll follow it up with some discussion about our own experiences with each piece of equipment or lack thereof.

Your list will vary from other cruisers' lists depending on what type of cruiser you have decided you want to be and what funds you have available. I don't think there is anyone that wouldn't prefer to have as many amenities as possible on a boat for comfort and safety's sake, but your cruising budget and the complexity of maintenance will determine what you're willing to do without. After doing this for a year and realizing that we are coastal cruisers and not blue water sailors, our equipment list would look much different now than when we were looking for the boat originally.

Item	Must	Ought	Wish
Electric Autopilot			
Windvane Steering			
Heat Pump			
Hot Water Heater			
VHF			
AIS			
SSB / Pactor Modem			
Sat Phone (con't)			

Item	Must	Ought	Wish
EPIRB			
Radar			
Chart Plotter			
Solar Panels			
Extra House Batteries			
Battery Monitor			
Wind Generator			
Diesel Generator			
Honda Generator			
Inverter			
Stove / Oven			
Microwave Oven			
Refrigerator			
Freezer			
Portable Freezer			
Foot Pump			
Water Maker			
LED Lighting			
TV / Stereo System (con't)			

Item	Must	Ought	Wish
Electric Head			
Dodger / Bimini			
Full Enclosure			
Life Raft			
Safety Equipment			
Dinghy			
Dinghy Motor			
Outboard Lift			
Dinghy Davits			
Bosun's Chair / Mast Climbing			
Electric Winches			
Electric Windlass			
Manual Windlass			
Anchor / Extra Anchor			
Communication Headsets (Marriage Savers)			
Dual Bow Roller			
Sails			
Roller Furling			
Removable Inner Stay and Running Backs (con't)			

Item	Must	Ought	Wish
Whisker Pole			
Spinnaker and Gear			
Deck Washdown Pump			
Outdoor Shower			

Electric Autopilot / Wind Vane Steering

Probably the number one thing that we purchased that we would have done differently was the windvane steering system. The boat ad included "autopilot" in the equipment list, but like so many things on our boat, it didn't function. We began to look into steering vanes. The idea of having a steering system that could operate without power was intoxicating, especially since we didn't have solar power on board. The Cape Horn was a nice-looking clean installation that would fit on our stern. They were known to be much more reliable, and electric autopilots were not. Most cruisers with electric autopilots carry at least one spare unit. At an average of $3,000-$4,000 per unit, an autopilot with a backup system was out of the question, so we took the plunge and installed the steering vane. As with many of the mistakes we made on this boat purchase, I was the driving force behind the steering vane. While most of the mistakes we made were things that we could live with and weren't that big of a deal, the lack of an electric autopilot has come back to us over and over. When the Cape Horn works well, it's a dream. We are sluicing along through the water using no power, a sweet thing indeed. The problem is that the learning curve is very steep and its uses are limited for the coastal cruiser. A steering vane is designed for open water sailing where you are weeks on the same tack in the same wind conditions. When coastal cruising, you are tacking more frequently and are subjected to rapidly shifting wind patterns or no wind at all. Not the best use for a steering vane. Additionally, they are unable to work with no wind or when the motor is running unless you install a tiller pilot to operate the wind vane which, in turn, operates the rudder. The installation is completely custom for each boat and can be time consuming. Even with the additional power requirements and the additional, and often badly timed, maintenance, the electric autopilot would have been the better

76

choice for us. Now that we're in the second year of cruising, we're becoming more comfortable with the wind vane and are successfully using it more often, but an electric tiller pilot to steer the boat while we're motoring will be a mandatory installation on our next haulout.

Heat Pump / Air Conditioning

Another ad item, "heat pump" was also non-functioning. The air conditioning part of the unit worked well, a fact that saved us the three summers we worked on the boat on Carlyle where the thermometer routinely hovers in the 100°-110° range in July and August with not even a stitch of breeze. The unit was a reverse cycle Mermaid Marine heat pump, an industry standard, and after realizing the reversing switch was the culprit and that the new switch was going to cost about $10 less than a whole new unit, we decided to toss the thing when we were ready to leave. Our decision was based on two major reasons. 1) We needed the closet space for my Sailrite sewing machine and clothes. Closet space is horribly limited on our boat and the heat pump unit and associated duct work took up the entire largest closet on the boat. 2) The unit only ran on 110 power which would require being on a dock to use it and we were not expecting to be on a dock for any great length of time. We've revisited the decision a few times, especially in light of the three months we spent on the dock in the killer heat of Ft. Lauderdale this past summer, but we would not have done anything differently here. We simply needed the space. We were able to purchase a portable heat pump for the summer that worked quite well and since it is also a heater and dehumidifier we can plug it in while the generator is on just to take the chill off or suck out some of the condensation. It is rather large and unwieldy, but it fits in a corner of the aft cabin so, for now, it's a good fit.

Hot Water Heater

Like most cruising boats in the 40-foot range, *Kintala* is outfitted with a six gallon aluminum hot water heater. It's anchored toward the center of the boat directly under the forward edge of the cockpit. It's about 12 feet from the galley sink and about 30 feet from the head fixtures. It takes a little over a gallon of running water to have the hot water reach the faucet in the head. Even if we both take our showers at the same time, a gallon a day times seven days a week times four weeks a month is a lot of wasted water. We tried containing it in a jug to use for flushing the head, which worked well, but since we have a Lavac head that only uses three pints to flush, we still couldn't use all of the water. It also required thirty minutes of the high throttle setting on the Honda generator to heat the six gallons of water, a noise level I have a difficult time living with. All of this is leading up to telling you that our solution for the moment has been to heat water in the tea kettle on the stove which we put in a collapsible wash basin and take a shower by pouring water over us from a cup. With this system we use very little power to heat the water, we waste no water getting the hot to the fixture, and our total water consumption is about a gallon each for a shower. The surprising thing? I rarely miss long hot showers. I really thought I would since I was in the habit of taking twenty minute long steaming hot showers when we lived in our condo. It turns out that the reason I needed those twenty minute showers was to try to get the knots out of my shoulders and ease the headache that I was getting from a job I didn't like. Job gone? Long hot shower not necessary. Don't get me wrong, when we're on land I do make use of the shower facilities, but I really don't miss it when we're on anchor. The ideal solution, and one we may eventually install, is a cockpit hot/cold faucet directly above the water heater or a solar water heating panel.

VHF, AIS, SSB, Sat Phone, EPIRB

So many electronics...so little money. As a former pilot, Tim would love to have all the electronic goodies possible but, alas, our cruising budget doesn't allow for so many toys. You might wonder why I've lumped all these things together. They are all safety-related communications devices and at some point you will have to decide which ones you will include.

Our VHF was old and *huge* so we pulled it out and bought a Standard Horizon GX2150 VHF/AIS combination at the boat show right before we left. While the AIS doesn't transmit, the receiver has been a godsend on our overnight trips. We've had the opportunity to identify and contact large ships in the shipping lanes, ships that could not see us even after we identified ourselves and gave our position. I would not sail anywhere without at least an AIS receiver. The transmitters are coming down in price exponentially every year, and if you can afford one I would highly recommend it. Our VHF also includes DSC (Digital Select Calling) capability, a much misunderstood and very little used option. Digital Select Calling allows you to directly contact another boat via their MMSI ship's radio registration number. This allows you to contact friends without hogging channel 16 to make the connection, also preventing every boat in the area from switching to your working channel and following your conversation. While it doesn't insure total privacy to your

78

communications, it does limit the community participation in it when not desired. Once you get your cruising yacht, you can arrange to practice using DSC with a friend until you're comfortable. Channel 16 is badly abused these days by boaters with no proper training in its use. Using DSC helps to clean up the channel, restoring it to its original purpose, international hailing and distress.

We had purchased a used SSB from a friend ours while we were still at the lake with the intention of installing it. This was another one of the blue-water-sailor driven purchases. We needed to be able to email our family when we were out of the range of cell towers, something we thought we would frequently need. We wanted to be able to post to our blog as well. We had also been told that the SSB would be a great source for weather when we were away from WiFi and cell reception, through the various weather guru broadcasts and cruiser nets. We ran out of time to do the complex installation so we stowed the boxes under the nav station and headed out with the intention to install it along the way somewhere. After many months of cruising, we discovered that we were rarely out of range of cell towers or WiFi, and for those times we purchased a DeLorme InReach unit. We chose the InReach because it has a real screen on it, unlike the SPOT, and it has real-time satellite two-way texting capacity, eliminating the need for a Sat Phone. The Sat Phone subscriptions were just too costly for our budget, although Iridium is now offering a reasonable phone/data package that will begin to change things. The InReach unit sends tracking information out to your recipients at whatever interval you specify, and has various monthly plans that allow unlimited preset messages which you can define like, "Leaving for our trip. Hoping for fair winds!" and "Delayed but doing fine. Don't worry." It also updates to social media like Facebook and in addition to the preset messages has an allotted number of included two-way text messages per month of up to 140 characters per message. Most models can also be paired to a smart phone to make the texting easier.

Safety equipment is a highly personal matter and what is right for us may not be right for you. I've included the EPIRB in this section but we've decided not to have one on our boat. We keep our InReach by the helm and, should we need to abandon the boat, it will be one of the first things we grab on the way off the boat. It has an SOS function that connects you to whomever you specify and, with the two-way texting function, allows you to communicate in real time with your potential rescuers. It is one of the best pieces of equipment that we purchased. Should you purchase a boat with an existing EPIRB or choose to buy one, be sure that the unit is registered and that the batteries are current. If you are purchasing an older boat that has an existing EPIRB, be sure that it is the newer 406 MHz model as the older frequencies are no longer monitored. Before you laugh and say that no current cruising boat would have such an outdated model, *Kintala* still had a Loran mounted on board when we purchased her in spite of the fact that Loran had not been supported since February of 2010. It was the first thing we threw in the dumpster when we started the refit. An option to a full-sized EPIRB are the newer PLBs (Personal Locating Beacons) that attach to your life vests. They are smaller and more readily available, as long as you remember to attach them to your vest. The cost can be greater, though, if you need to purchase two units for Captain and crew. Whatever options you choose, be sure that they are current, powered, and registered.

Radar / Chart Plotter

Radar would be number one on the former pilot wish list. We do have a small chart plotter at the helm, but it does not include radar. Tim is extremely proficient at using the radar after 13,000 hours of flying and consistently feels like he is blind because he can't see weather ahead of us when we're out of range of cell radar. Since radar is still out of our budget reach, we have alleviated this lack somewhat this season by buying a portable shortwave radio with SSB channels on it that can receive the weather fax tones. The iPad has an app called HF Weather Fax by Black Cat that will interpret those tones through the iPad microphone and turn them into a weather fax on screen. $200 investment vs. $3,000. That also gives us the ability to listen to the various weather gurus on the SSB channels even though we can't transmit, and gives us entertainment in the form of international radio shows we enjoy like BBC.

In regards to the various chart plotters and NMEA connections: if we had a newer boat we would absolutely have a coordinated NMEA connection between all of our instruments and our computers. The complexity and expense of install isn't justified on an old boat like this so we have opted to use our small Garmin helm chart plotter as a backup and our two iPads as primary navigation. We have Garmin Bluechart Mobile and Navionics+ on both of the iPads. We keep one plugged in and one with us under the dodger, both in waterproof cases. The batteries last 14 hours, even checking them pretty frequently. We use the Garmin Bluechart because it has Active Captain[6] data that you can view offline.

---

6 Activecaptain.com is a crowd- sourced navigation aid that provides bridge information, marina, mooring, and anchorage information as well as user reviews on each of those. It also offers hazard warnings updated recently by the members, and the eboatcard system to social network.

The bridge, marina, and anchorage information is invaluable. Navionics is a bit more user-friendly, especially with its distance measuring and route planning, but it's not as reliable on charts in the Bahamas. This is changing, however, with the Navionics Sonar Charts, a crowd-sourced program of updating depths through the purchase of one of their Sonar Phones. You install it on your boat and it transmits the depth information where you cruise. The updated information is then applied to the Navionics charts within a few days. Both Garmin Blue Chart and Navionics are pretty inexpensive and you can get them for iOS or Android, for tablets or phones. There are also other apps out there that work with Active Captain. You can find them on their website, www.activecaptain.com. You can't have enough backup when it comes to navigation. We have 2 iPads, 4 laptops, 2 stand-alone GPS units and 2 smart phones, all with navigation software on them. If you're pretty computer literate you can try Open CPN, an open source navigation program for laptops. If you decide to purchase iPads, don't waste your money on the newer iPad Air or even generation 3 or 4. The gen 2 iPads function perfectly with both programs and can be had for a fraction of the price on Amazon.com. Just be sure that you purchase the 3G capable version because it has the stand-alone GPS. You don't need a carrier subscription with it, just that model. One word of caution on any iOS product: don't be the first to install a software update and never, ever, do one while depending on the iPad for navigation support on a cruise. Many of the software updates in recent history have caused navigation products to malfunction and have left cruisers high and dry. Let others do the initial testing for you.

Power Generation and Battery Monitoring

Ahhh...to have a magic boat that draws power out of the air and the sun. As a good friend of ours suggested recently, we might have been better off when setting up our boat to leave out the steering vane and buy solar and wind with the same money. While we've since become better friends with the steering vane, his point was well-taken. Today solar is a viable option because panels are increasing in efficiency and dropping in price like ten tons of lead brick. Just four years ago, that wasn't the case. Enough solar power to maintain our boat without using supplemental power generation would have cost us about $5,000 at the time. We had no place to put rigid panels with their associated weight, and the semi-flexes were just coming out at a whopping $1,250 per 125 watts. Through some very odd series of circumstances we ended up with two 100-watt newish panels to install and we have been simply shocked at how efficient they are. Our electric demand is actually much less than we had estimated and we have been able to run our generator a fraction of the time we needed to before the solar installation.

Wind generation is something we are considering as our next addition to the power-producing arsenal. There are some smaller, less expensive generators coming out that we have seen installed on cruising boats and are also in our budget range. While they are not as sophisticated or as efficient as some of the more common marine wind generators, they may allow entry into the wind generation market for budget cruisers. More research will certainly be needed, as well as a plan to develop some space on the stern to install a pole.

At the time we left and with the budget constraints, we decided to purchase the highly recommended Honda EU2000i Companion Model generator and it still remains one of the top most useful items we have on the boat. It starts every time, even after sitting for a while. It starts with one easy pull. It's light to carry. On cloudy days when the solar panels won't charge the batteries, it runs its happy little heart out for 5 hours and burns less than a half gallon a day doing it. It is the closest to magic that we could afford when we left to go cruising and we've been incredibly grateful to have it. One huge advantage to the Companion Model is that it has a 30 amp shore power cord outlet on the side into which you plug your boat shore power cord. This makes all the 110 volt outlets in the boat available the whole time you're running the generator. 110 volt power is one thing we rarely struggle with as a result of the Honda generator. We purchased an inverter, but along with several other items it had been tossed in the "install it next time we're on the hard" pile. With the recent addition of the solar panels that inverter install is getting bumped up the list, but its smallish size will mean that we will still need the generator to run my sewing machine and the shop vacuum. The inverter should handle the electronics charging like laptops and phones, and the occasional use of the Magic Bullet and the hand mixer, but I do canvas work to generate some extra cash on occasion, so there will be days that we are running the Honda even if the sun is charging the batteries. The Honda has had a side benefit as well of allowing us to purchase the much less expensive 110 volt appliances instead of the 12 volt ones that don't work as well. The batteries on both of our cordless drills failed in the first year out. Replacing the batteries costs nearly as much as buying a whole new drill and battery combination, so I think we'll stick with 110v drills.

The other generator option is a diesel generator. This boat came equipped with one from the factory, but at some point it was removed. I'm happy to have the storage space it left behind and happy also not to have the noise inside the boat. Were we buying a new boat, we would probably opt to have one but having one on this boat is not something I wish for.

Whatever power generation you choose, you will need to have adequate batteries to store the power and a means of monitoring those batteries. While you will find cruisers on all sides of the battery style debate, AGM batteries are without any doubt the safest. There is no need to ventilate them to the outside, and no need for routine maintenance. The batteries on *Kintala* are buried under the aft berth mattress, on top of which resides everything that would normally go in the cockpit locker that we don't have because of the narrow stern. If we had to check the water in wet batteries, it simply wouldn't get done as often. We were able to purchase some "seconds" AGM batteries from a vendor at the boat show, seconds only due to scratches on the cases which made them unable to be sold. We have gotten flawless performance from them in the eighteen months since we left and I would have no qualms about buying seconds again. They were literally a fraction of the price of new. Battery technology is advancing by leaps and bounds and, while I wouldn't risk the fire hazard of the new lithium batteries on our boat, I suspect that soon you will be able to double your capacity in the same space you currently use for batteries.

Galley Equipment and Water Delivery

Galley equipment is one of the most varied areas of equipment that you'll find on cruising boats. Some people like to spend their days on a dock and eat out at restaurants 3-5 days a week. Some people are happy to cook on a Coleman stove in the cockpit. The galley on *Kintala* was one of her most redeeming qualities. I had specifically wanted either an L-shaped or U-shaped galley for safety. The inline galleys that are so prevalent on newer cruising boats leave no place to stabilize yourself against when you are in a rough seaway or anchorage. For me, a good stove and oven are essential. I love to cook and I spend a lot of time in the galley. We have a propane stove and oven which are the closest to a home stove that is available on a boat. I have cooked with a non-pressurized alcohol stove on our previous boat and, while it did work, it wasn't very efficient. It never got hot enough to cook things like pizza. Whatever type you choose, keep in mind that cooking fuel has the greatest potential for injury and death on a boat of nearly everything else. Be sure to set good habits when handling fuel and install all the necessary safety equipment related to those fuels.

I've never felt the need to have a microwave on the boat. We really don't have the space but, if we did, I could see the benefits of having one. On a passage it would be good to be able to duck down and heat up a cup of soup right in the cup, saving both time and dish washing. There are also some who swear by them as a Faraday Cage for their electronics during a lightning storm, although I've read recently that they are only marginally effective for that purpose as the glass doors allow too much current to pass through.

Refrigeration is also one of those great debate items. Some people simply won't go cruising without one (we're in that category), and some simply won't have one aboard. Clearly, refrigeration is the highest energy demand on a boat. For some, the energy demand and maintenance issues outweigh the benefit. We decided that we had done enough camping in our lifetimes and didn't want to camp on our boat. We wanted a civilized home to live in, and refrigeration was a must. Refrigerators vary in size, orientation, shape and capacity. We have a top-loading refrigerator that used to include a partial freezer that has since been removed. The top-loading units are more efficient because you don't lose as much cold air every time you open them, but that efficiency comes with a price. It's very difficult to find things in them and you often find yourself removing half of the contents to find the item you were looking for. There are various methods of organizing the top-loader from baskets to bags.

We do not currently have a freezer on board. Our refrigerator is a 90s-vintage Adler-Barbour that is working well so we won't replace it until it fails. The plate for it is a wrap-around plate in an L shape that will freeze (and keep frozen) several packages of meat as long as they remain alongside the plate. The unit will also keep a 10# bag of ice frozen for as long as it takes us to use it, also as long as it's alongside the plate. The only thing it will not keep frozen is ice cream and if anything motivates us to buy a freezer it will likely be that. In all likelihood, we would buy a portable freezer unit like the Engel, just large enough for a few packages of frozen vegetables and some ice cream. The portable units are still quite expensive and are cost prohibitive to many, but they do provide an easy solution to the lack of refrigeration on some boats.

The last galley item to put some thought into is water delivery. Spend the money on a good water pressure pump that's quiet. It's a good $200 spent. We have a fresh water foot pump in the galley so that if the pressure pump breaks or we have a power failure we can still access our water tanks. We have three water tanks on board that run through a selection manifold. This prevents all of our water from being contaminated at the same time if we develop an issue. Some boats also have a salt water foot pump for rinsing dishes prior to washing them. I would like to have one, although there are a lot of places you will anchor that you would not want to use it due to the pollution in the water. We have a separate drinking water faucet that has an under-the-counter double filtration system. Water filtration systems are invaluable on a boat. We filter ours going into the tanks with Camco RV high flow filters, at the main manifold with the same filters, and at the drinking water faucet with the high pressure filters.

The final water delivery item is a water maker. There's much debate on the subject of water makers. While they do make you more independent from the dock, they are also horribly expensive and require a substantial amount of maintenance, some of which is also expensive. The thought is that you might want to choose smaller tanks and refill the tanks more frequently with a water maker. If you're going to have one, it must be used frequently or it must be pickled, so frequent use and smaller tankage makes sense. The difficulty arises when you are in a harbor where you can't make water, which is most of them. Harbors are rife with oil and gasoline pollution, overboard dumping of sewage, and farming contamination. What this means for you is that you will have to leave your anchorage to go outside the harbor to make water and you may lose your prime anchor real estate. Not a big deal if you're already needing to go outside to dump a holding tank; you just need to time the trips.

Lighting and Entertainment

One of the least expensive and easiest ways you can reduce your energy requirements on a boat is to replace all of the incandescent lights with LED. The warm white LED bulbs mimic the ambiance of incandescent lighting, are cool to the touch, and draw a tiny fraction of the power. You no longer even need to replace whole fixtures as there are drop-in LED bulbs that fit nearly every fixture on a boat. We had some very dark corners in the boat where we added LED strip lights. The difference in the interior was startling. You can buy strip lights that have dimmers on them as well. Just be sure to buy marine grade water resistant fixtures that will be less likely to corrode. While you're at it, don't forget to replace the navigation and mast head lighting with LED. Be sure to purchase Coast Guard approved LED bulbs for the navigation lights as some of the bulbs will render the green nav lights a bluish tint that is not legal. LED anchor lights are a much safer alternative as they can be seen much farther away.

In addition to LED cabin lighting, you may want some sort of entertainment system. Some boats come with stereo systems that have speakers throughout the boat and in the cockpit. Some come with flat screen TVs. It's totally a matter of your personal requirements. We don't watch TV and the occasional DVD we watch is done on a computer screen. We generally watch movies in the cockpit, placing the laptop on the cockpit table between the cockpit seats. We have talked about getting a flat screen with a built-in DVD player to mount in the V-berth at some point, but in the cooler weather we're quite pleased to be in the cockpit watching a movie with the backdrop of the sunset on the bay.

We use our iPads for music and we use a waterproof Bluetooth speaker with a suction cup that we take with us to the cockpit. A Bluetooth speaker lets you take it with you wherever you go, even to a dock for a potluck or sundowners. We like the portability of the iPad for music much better than a built-in system, but I know people who swear by their built-in stereo systems. I had purchased one early on but it sat in the box in the aft cabin for a year after which I sold it since we were quite happy with the iPad for entertainment. We are voracious readers and spend most of the time reading. Early on we both had Kindles but they do not seem to be up to the harsh marine environment and both of them quit working. We now use our iPads with a Kindle app to read.

Head Types

There are a few typical types of heads found on most boats. The basic Jabsco model that has a plunger-type pump handle is found on more small cruising yachts and weekend sailors than probably any other brand. They are inexpensive, easy to install, and repair parts are readily available. The biggest drawback to them is the fact that the joker valve requires frequent replacement. Also, if you do not remember to flip the flush/dry switch you can flood and sink the boat if your anti-siphon valve fails (and they do, often).

Beyond the basic Jabsco, there is the vacuum head of which the most well-known is the Lavac. This is the type of head on *Kintala*, one we installed soon after buying the boat because the one that resided there previously was (surprise) not working. The Lavac heads use very little water, emit very little odor due to the rubber vacuum seals on both the lid and the seat, and rarely break. The pumps are robust and with different plumbing options can be set up to pump overboard and to be used as a spare bilge pump. They come in manual and electric and, while they are more expensive than the Jabsco, they are still quite reasonable.

As you move into the realm of more complexity, there is the Electra-San. This head uses an electrical charge to treat the sewage before pumping it overboard. It is legal to discharge this treated sewage in all coastal waters except for those areas specifically designated as no-discharge zones. Having this head would relieve you of much of the pump-out hassles but, as with all things on a boat, it comes with a cost. The initial unit is quite pricey, it uses a great amount of electricity which often requires a separate battery, and the maintenance is demanding as well as aesthetically unpleasant.

You might elect to go with a composting head. The initial cost is about average for heads, there are no power or pump-out requirements, and there is no thru-hull requirement, but there are several disadvantages. You still have to empty the liquid container periodically, if you have more than two people on board the solids often do not compost fast enough or completely enough, and they are prone to acquiring bugs in the warmer climes.

Some boats have more than one head. It is commonplace in boats with more than one head to see one of them plumbed to empty directly overboard and the other to go into a holding tank. When sailing in an area outside the three-mile limit the overboard head is used, and when inside the three-mile limit the holding tank head is used. Some two-head boats will fit a composting head in one and a standard head in the other to give them more options. Be sure to check the regulations for the waters in which you want to cruise. In most U.S. Waters, if you are boarded by the Coast Guard, you will need to show proof that your overboard Y-valve is locked out, preventing discharge. Whatever system you choose, you can expect to be changing out the system to fit your personal lifestyle.

Dodger / Bimini / Full Enclosure

It is very rare to find a used cruising boat that is not fitted with at least a bimini, and most are fitted with a dodger to cover the companionway entrance. A few come outfitted with a full enclosure of screen or plastic or both. It is not possible to emphasize the importance of these items. Excess sun will simply wear you out in the tropics, and cold, wind and rain will wear you out in the northern cruising grounds. If you find yourself doing many anchor watches from the cockpit without the protection of a sturdy dodger, your cruising plans will likely come to an abrupt end. If your used cruising boat is not outfitted with a bimini and dodger at a bare minimum, make plans to spend $4,000-$5,000 to outfit the boat with them. If you are accomplished at sewing you can build both a bimini and dodger for half that price but you will have 50-100 hours invested in labor. The dodger that we constructed for *Kintala* is still number one on our effort-to-reward list for projects completed.

Safety Equipment

Life Vests	Flares
Fire Extinguishers	First Aid Kit
Publications / Placards	Propane Solenoid
Propane Regulator	Propane Sniffer
Smoke Detectors	CO Detectors
Bilge Blower	EPIRB
Ditch Bag	SPOT or InReach Communicator
Man Overboard Pole	Personal Locating Beacons
Jacklines	Tethers
Lifelines	Life Sling

As mentioned in the previous section on electronics, safety equipment is a highly personal issue. Some safety items are certainly required by the Coast Guard, but many more are elective. At a minimum, you will be required to carry fire extinguishers that are Coast Guard approved and of the required type, day signals such as flags, night signals such as flares, life jackets, and a throwable device. There are also requirements for placards and publications that must be on the boat. The required items are out of the scope of this book and vary by the length of your boat. You can read the requirements at the USCGboating.org website. Common sense dictates that you carry a well-equipped first aid kit beefed up with some antibiotics, dental repair items, suturing supplies and splints. As a coastal cruiser you will rarely be very far from some sort of medical assistance but if you travel the outlying areas or are a true blue water cruiser, you must be able and equipped to do at least the minimum care.

Tip →→ *Be sure to check the minimum required safety equipment list for your vessel at: www.uscgboating.org*

Beyond the minimum requirements, you may elect to carry a life raft if you're going off shore. Life rafts are expensive to purchase and cost upwards of 60% of the purchase price to have them recertified in 2 years. Many people refuse to travel without them and others choose not to have them. The data surrounding life raft deployment and successful rescue is almost non-existent so making a decision about a life raft will be one of the most painful ones you will make. Do your homework, make a decision, and then accept the consequences. The ad for *Kintala* included a life raft. It was out of date on the certification and when we took it to the facility to have it recertified we were informed that they would be unable to do it. The unit required to activate the life raft is no longer available so if they deployed it they would be unable to repack it. A new one is near $2,000 for a basic model, so be sure to account for this in your offer on your boat. If it's expired, assume it's no good.

If your galley includes a propane stove, you cannot devote enough time and attention to the safety items related to it. There must be a dedicated propane locker outside the living area and it must be vented overboard. Propane is heavier than air and will find its way to the bottom of the bilge where it will lie in wait for the first opportunistic spark. Every year we hear about a boat exploding or catching fire. A good propane system will include a pressure leak test gauge on the tanks, a solenoid inside the galley to shut off the propane, blow-out protection on the burners to shut off the gas in the event the flame is blown out, a propane sniffer, and a bilge blower. The blower is run 5 minutes before running the engine to vent any fumes overboard.

Smoke detectors and CO detectors must be of marine quality or they will constantly give false alarms that may cause you to ignore a real one. (Regular house units are terribly susceptible to humidity and moisture, both of which are in abundance inside a cruising boat.) Placing *any* detectors, marine quality or not, can present a challenge. Finding a location sufficiently distant from motors, engines, or gas sources in a small boat is difficult at best. Keep at it. It's worth the effort.

The last eight items on the list are all devoted to the need for evacuation from the boat or dealing with a man overboard situation. As previously discussed in the electronics section, we have elected to carry a DeLorme InReach instead of an EPIRB. Some people are electing to carry Personal Locating Beacons, or PLBs. The PLBs are slightly less expensive than an EPIRB but you must have one for each crew member as they are attached to your life vest. Some models include a GPS and can pinpoint the location down to a few meters. For more information visit the NOAA site: http://www.sarsat.noaa.gov/emerbcns.html.

We often joke that there are only two safety rules on our boat:

1) Keep the water out of the boat.

2) Keep the people in the boat.

There are many safety items to aid you in accomplishing the latter, hopefully negating the need for some of the search and rescue aids. Most cruising boats have a set of jacklines, flat high-strength webbing that hooks on the bow and stern of your boat and lays on your deck onto which you clip a tether. Some cruisers simply use a good rope, but rope is hard on the feet and can be slippery. Some run them over the cabin top to limit the distance to fall. Spend the money on a good set of tethers. They come in single tethers that hook to your harness or D-ring equipped life vest and then clip to the jackline. Some come with a Y-shaped tether that gives you the opportunity to unclip one and clip it around an obstruction like a side stay before unclipping the other one. Again, personal preference. We have made a promise to each other that we will *never* leave the safety of the companionway without clipping on our tether at night or in rough seas. We also have a rule that no one goes forward out of the cockpit at night without the other person in the cockpit. Whatever jackline and tether system you use, inspect it frequently. It will do you no good to have them if a wave sends you over the lifeline and the worn stitching on your tether picks that particular moment to fail. Be sure that whatever fastener you hook your jacklines and tethers to have sufficient backing plates to handle the load. An average 175 pound adult being flung off the boat is an unbelievable amount of force, enough to put you right through the lifelines. While on the subject of lifelines, I will emphasize what Tim has already mentioned previously: if you have the plastic coated lifelines on the boat, throw them away and get either plain stainless wire or Dyneema to replace them. Corrosion lurks beneath the plastic coating, corrosion that you will never know is there until you need the lifeline and it fails.

When all else fails and you have decided to abandon ship, a ditch bag that has been previously prepared should be your first item to grab. The contents of a ditch bag alone can break your cruising kitty to bits, so research it, talk about it, agree on the contents and assemble it. Some things you might include are a spare VHF, a spare GPS, flashlights, extra batteries, your passports, wallets, cellphones, boat documents and insurance information, water, some granola bars, sunscreen, flares, small notebook and pencil, and a small first aid kit. If you are using your dinghy as a life raft, something that many people do who can't afford an official life raft, you may want to include items like fishing gear, signaling mirror, binoculars, dinghy repair kit, MREs, and a hand-held water maker. Remember that a ditch bag is only as good as its accessibility and currency. Expiration dates of consumables need to be checked on a regular basis. Finding that you have no charged batteries for your shortwave radio after you're in the liferaft would be disheartening.

Kintala sports a LifeSling2 on her stern, a piece of equipment designed to retrieve a crew member from the water once you locate them. It is comprised of a U-shaped foam flotation device attached to line which is then attached to the boat. Its purpose is to aid you in the retrieval of a crew from the water after you've located them. To use it, you throw the LifeSling2 off the boat and the person in the water slips it around them, allowing you to hoist them into the boat via some tackle on the boom. Although, thankfully, we've never had to deal with a man overboard situation, the LifeSling2 would enable the remaining crew on board to lift a person whom they would not be able to lift otherwise. The Boat U.S. Foundation prepared some statistics on man overboard incidents for the years 2003 through 2007. Of the 3,133 boating deaths during those five years, 749 were due to a man overboard situation. Here are their statistics[7]:

- 24% were characterized as falls overboard

- 24% died at night, 76% died in daytime

- 82% were on a boat under 22ft in length

- 63% did not know how to swim

- Only 8% of non–swimmers were wearing life jackets

- 90% occurred when weather conditions were calm or had less than 1-foot chop

- Just 4% of the boats had two engines

- 85% of fatalities were men

- Average age was 47 (con't)

7   Chris Edmonston, President of Boat U.S. Foundation

- During the day, alcohol consumption played a part in 27% of the deaths

- At night, alcohol played a part in 50% of the deaths

- Falling overboard while fishing - 41% of the deaths

While it's plain to see that the majority of man overboard situations are not on cruising yachts, there simply is no substitute for careful planning and preparation as well as firm rules which are never broken to keep all crew on board, eliminating the need to rescue someone.

The selection of additional safety equipment is limited only by your space to contain it and your budget to pay for it. Unfortunately, vendors of safety items know how to prey on your fears and will make you feel that you simply must have all of their wares. See what's available, match it against your budget, and decide what compromises you can live with.

Dinghy and Related Handling

Cruisers all talk about the fact that the dinghy is your family car. There are as many opinions about the correct type of dinghy as there are opinions on what the best family car is. The reality is that very few people choose their initial dinghy since a good many cruising boats come equipped with one of the previous owner's choosing. There are four basic types: inflatables which are manufactured from either PVC or Hypalon material; rigid inflatables, which have a hard fiberglass bottom with attached inflatable tubes; hard dinghies made from fiberglass, aluminum, or wood; and folding or nesting dinghies made from fiberglass, wood, or flexible materials of various types. Each type has pros and cons and, should you have the opportunity to purchase one of your own choosing, research ahead of time will help you to end up with the dinghy that works best for you.

Dinghy Type	Pros	Cons
Rollable inflatable with either an air floor or slat floor made from wood or aluminum	Lightweight, inexpensive, stores in a smaller footprint when not in use	Not very durable, can be difficult to get in and out of air floor models. Can be difficult to store if the floor is slatted, easy to damage on rocks & coral

Dinghy Type	Pros	Cons
Rigid Inflatable (RIB)- a dinghy with a rigid fiberglass bottom and inflatable tubes	Easy to maneuver, easy to board, more stable when standing, accepts a bigger motor, planes with bigger motor, not easily damaged on rocky shores or coral	Much heavier, difficult to stow on the foredeck, more expensive
Hard dinghy – like a Walker Bay with fixed seats	More interior space, easier to row, planes with bigger motor, not easily damaged on rocks or coral, may have flotation chambers, sailing kits	More difficult to stow on the foredeck, more expensive
Folding or nesting dinghy like a Port-a-Bote	Take less room to store, some are more stable to stand in	More expensive, takes time to assemble, more individual parts to keep track of

The choice of a motor for the dinghy depends largely on how you plan to cruise. If you plan on spending most of your time at anchor and would like to spend that time in more remote areas then you will want a bigger motor so you can get to shore which can sometimes be over a mile away. A larger engine is also a good idea if you plan on using the dinghy to fish from or to explore with. If you have a larger crew, say two adults and two teenagers, then a larger dinghy with a 15hp motor is very nearly an absolute necessity. What capacity you have to lift the motor is also a consideration. If you have a motor lift then a bigger motor is a possibility. On *Kintala* we have a 3.5hp Mercury 4-stroke which weighs in at 35 pounds. We don't have a motor lift so it was important that I be able to lift the motor by myself. In spite of the fact that everyone told us we *had* to have a 15hp motor, we have rarely wished for a bigger motor. In fact, Tim recently hurt his back and was unable to lift the motor at all. Had we caved in to conventional wisdom and bought the larger motor, I would have been unable to launch the dinghy myself. It would be nice, though, to have a motor that will vacuum feed from a large gas tank through a hose and ours does not. It holds only a half gallon of gasoline so if we want to take a longer tour of an anchorage we frequently have to stop and fill the tank.

Many people swear by their 2-stroke engines. They seem to start more reliably, are generally much easier to obtain parts for in foreign countries, and their parts are generally less expensive. The one big drawback on the 2-stroke is the environmental factor. They are noisy and tend to smoke a lot. There are electric motors like the Torqueedo, and propane motors, both of which have advantages and disadvantages and neither of which we have any experience with. As with the dinghy itself, most use whatever came with the boat until it no longer functions and needs replaced.

Accessories for dinghies are a long list of their own. Some boats come installed with davits to raise and store the dinghy behind the boat. While this is extremely convenient and also minimizes dinghy theft, it can throw the weight of your boat off balance and effect the handling of it. Davits have also been known to break a time or two in rough weather. They can be a tremendous advantage for older crew for whom getting a dinghy on deck can be a challenge. Most davits have at least a 2:1 purchase on the raising tackle, and some a 4:1 advantage, making it much easier to lift it out of the water.

A motor lift is fairly inexpensive and easy to install and is relatively low impact to the space on most sterns. *Kintala* sports a very narrow stern and, as a result, is sans motor lift. The stern is already cluttered enough with the steering vane and Life Sling. Motor lifts allow a single person to mount and dismount the outboard on the dinghy. It's a great benefit to single-handed or short-handed crews.

For the dinghy itself, you will need life jackets, oars, a gas can of some sort, and a dinghy anchor. It's amazing how quickly an inflatable dinghy can be carried away in a current. A lot of anchorages are close to inlets to the open sea and should you lose your motor you could be carried out to sea before anyone could assist you. Some form of communication is required by the Coast Guard as well. A whistle is sufficient but we always carry either a hand held VHF or a cell phone in waterproof containers. At night you are required to have an all-around white light in the rear and red and green lights on the bow. Most cruisers use the suction cup lights that adhere to the top of the outboard for the white light and a hand held flashlight style red-green nav light for the bow. If your dinghy is inflatable you'll need an air pump and a good repair kit with 2-part glue that's specific to your dinghy type. PVC repair kits are not interchangeable with Hypalon repair kits. If you're planning on towing your dinghy behind the boat then you will need a tow harness made from some sort of floating line or webbing. If you're planning on using your dinghy as a platform from which to snorkel or dive then a dinghy ladder is essential. If you don't believe me, try to get back into your dinghy some time by yourself. Be sure to have the main ladder deployed on your boat so you can get back onto the boat when you realize you can't get into the dinghy by yourself.

Line Handling Equipment

If you intend to sail your sailboat, one of the first things you will have to check on any boat you're interested in buying is the line handling equipment: winches, traveler, rope clutches, cleats, chocks. Winches should be oversized for the size of boat and all of the clutches, cleats and chocks should be heavily back-plated. Whatever cleats hold your anchor snubber should be particularly heavy duty since they hold the entire force of the anchor when it is deployed. Check all of the sheaves on the entire boat to see that they are not worn or cracked, including the ones at the top of the mast. Delrin sheaves, or aluminum ones for that matter, are extremely expensive and many times have to be custom made on older boats. Look for wear in the running rigging that will offer telltale hints about the line handling equipment. How much line handling equipment your boat needs will be determined in part by whether you opt to lead all of the control lines back to the cockpit. There are good reasons to do so, and there are people who choose not to. *Kintala* was equipped to do so, but we ended up routing things back to the mast because the cockpit area is so small that it was hopelessly cluttered with that arrangement and made it more dangerous than going forward to deal with the sails. If your crew is older or you are short-handed, an electric winch or two can be a life saver. Portable electric winches like the WinchRite may be a good option for your crew. They can certainly be essential for sending someone up the mast, which leads me to the final item in this section: mast climbing equipment. There are many options available to climb the mast: foldable steps, webbing ladders, conventional climbing gear, and the bosun's chair. Most of the time something (and the people to help) can be borrowed when you need to go up the mast, so don't stress too much about this type of equipment.

Tip →→ Be sure there are enough halyards on the boat to secure a main line and a safety line to whatever harness you are using to climb the mast.

Anchoring Equipment

Anchoring equipment is the single most important thing you will buy. Quality ground tackle is expensive, so if your boat is already well-equipped, this will significantly reduce the costs associated with refitting your cruising boat. Every boat you consider must be either well-equipped or you must budget for it.

As far as the type of anchor goes, this is one of those topics that will spark high-spirited arguments in cruiser circles, everyone swearing by the one he or she has. The new generation anchors such as the Rocna, Manson Supreme, or Mantus are clearly proving themselves to be at the top of the stack. *Kintala* sports a 65# Mantus on the bow and we sleep peacefully.

An electric windlass is on every cruiser's wish list. Some are lucky enough to get a boat with one installed. An electric windlass is a pretty important piece of equipment for single-handers and older crew. They also make you more likely to re-anchor if the first placement was not optimal, where with a manual windlass or no windlass at all you might be tempted to say, "Oh, it'll be OK" even if it's not ideal. The disadvantages are high power use and the tendency to break at the most inconvenient times.

Cruisers have endless expert opinions on anchoring equipment and its use. You have to decide for yourself and you will hopefully have the opportunity to use some different anchors on other people's boats and charter boats before you commit. We started out with a 59# CQR and it dragged incessantly. Taking the plunge to buy the Mantus was some of the best money we spent.

The miscellaneous things that we've learned about anchoring equipment over the first year of cruising are (in no special order):

- Buy oversized. If the manufacturer's application chart shows a 40# anchor works for a 35-40 foot boat and you have a 40-foot boat, buy the next sized anchor. If *Kintala* had an electric windlass, she would even be sporting a 100# anchor instead of a 65#, which was already oversized.

- For the most part, you will rarely need more than 100 feet of chain while cruising in the Florida and Bahamas areas. 100 feet of chain spliced to 200 feet of nylon rode will do well for most of your cruising unless you cruise the deeper waters of New England or the Pacific Northwest. If you have the room and the weight capacity to handle 250-300 feet of chain in the bow, then have at it. If you can afford it, buy the High Test chain and go one size smaller to save on weight.

- CQR style anchors don't work very well in grass which is everywhere in the Bahamas. It's almost comical watching people try to set them there.

- Rig a good anchor snubber out of 3-strand nylon and use it every time you set the anchor.

- No anchor is worth anything if it's not set properly. Back slowly as the chain is let out to avoid making a pile of chain. Set the anchor well in reverse.

- Don't forget to add the distance from the water to your bow into your scope calculations. Also remember the tide changes and add that depth to your scope calculations. Depth of the water + distance to bow + tide X scope = anchor rode length. Example: 7 feet of water depth + 4 feet to the bow + 2 foot tide = 13ft X 6:1 scope = 78 feet of rode. Scope will change with the wind and current and how crowded the anchorage is.

- Full duplex 2-way communication headsets are worth gold on a cruising boat. Being able to communicate in a normal speaking voice when docking or anchoring or any other high-stress time of communication is bumping your chance for success up a few notches. Besides, it makes the anchorage more pleasant for everyone else who now doesn't have to listen to your screaming. Ours have recently quit working and we are now using a whistle signal system, but we are comfortable doing that only because we used the headsets for so long and learned what each of us needed for a successful anchoring experience.

- A spare anchor is a good thing to have. You never know when a power boat will snag your rode and you'll have to cut the anchor line and let the anchor go. You can always come back and dive for it later, but you need a spare anchor in the mean time. Choosing a different style for your spare, such as a lightweight Danforth that stores easily, is a good idea. You will see many cruising boats with a dual bow roller and two anchors permanently mounted on the bow. Unfortunately *Kintala's* bow is too narrow for such a configuration.

Sails, Furlers, and Related Gear

There are some affordable older cruising boats out there that still have hanked-on sails although roller furling is clearly the standard. Especially for short-handed and older crews, the roller-furled sail is points in the safety bucket. Not having to go forward to deploy or change a sail can mean not falling off the boat. While roller-furled mainsails have been slow to be accepted due to jamming problems in the early years, many cruising boats are fitted with either an in-mast furling system or an in-boom furling system for the mainsail. Whichever way you choose to go, be sure that the system is functioning flawlessly. Check the operation of all furling systems both at the dock and under sail. *Kintala* had suffered some severe damage a few years before we bought her and the damaged furler had been replaced with an undersized (and, yes, cheaper) model. Not having any previous experience with roller furling, we had no idea that the difficulty we had in furling the sail was because it wasn't the correct size. We fought with that thing constantly before a rigger told us what was wrong and we changed it out for the properly sized unit.

Tip → → *Don't ever assume that something was done correctly on a boat even if it was done by a reputable shop. It's your safety in the balance and no one cares about your safety as much as you do.*

A cutter rig with an inside stay can add tremendous flexibility to your sailing configurations. Some boats are outfitted with a removable stay which requires the addition of running back stays to offset the pull on the mast. Others are permanent. On many boats, the staysail can be sheeted inside the stays and make it possible to sail much closer to the wind. It can also give you the option of furling to a very small sail area for heavy winds.

Sails are quite probably the most overlooked item when considering a cruising boat. All that a potential buyer wants to see is that there *are* sails. If the sails are deteriorating due to UV damage, and if they have been restitched as many times as is possible, then new sails will be on your refit list. In the case of *Kintala*, the mainsail was missing altogether. The previous owner had destroyed the sail on a very windy Chicago day just prior to laying up the boat for the winter and our subsequent purchase of her. In many ways that was a huge blessing to us. We were forced to buy a new mainsail, something we would not have done if there had been any sail there at all. We purchased a U.K. Halsey main with a

Tides Marine Strong Track System, a system that allows me to hoist the main by myself, something I would have been unable to do with a standard main. Replacing just the main and one jib on a typical 40-foot cruising boat will run somewhere either side of $10,000 in 2015 dollars.

Sail decisions are intimately tied to the "What type of cruiser are you?" section. If you want to be able to go down the entire length of the ICW in the late fall, then you will want a shorter rig that can fit under all the bridges, even the Julia Tuttle bridge north of Miami which is 56 feet instead of the standard 65 feet. This may call for a ketch rig for you. A ketch rig has huge advantages for sail choice. The sails are smaller, lighter weight, easier to hoist and easier to remove and stow. There are more choices of configurations to balance the boat in heavier weather as well. We had never been particularly fond of the look of a ketch rig, but the astounding number of these boats in the cruiser community is a clear indication of the benefits they provide.

Kintala came with six sails: two genoas, two staysails, a reacher and a spinnaker. We added the new mainsail for a total of seven. After sailing her for over four years and one of those years cruising, it has become apparent to us that we really only need three: a main, a genoa, a staysail and possibly a spare genoa in the event that we tear the one on the roller. *Kintala* sails so well on just the genoa that we have found ourselves spending way over two-thirds of our sailing time with just that one sail up. The reality of it is that we will never hoist a spinnaker with just the two of us to handle it, and there is absolutely zero chance we would change out the roller genoa for the reacher unless we were making a month-long passage across the Pacific. It's simply too dangerous on the narrow, cluttered foredeck of our boat to make that kind of sail change. We have found that a whisker pole is essential to hold the genoa out full when the wind is light. It usually adds close to a knot to our speed, something we just can't give up when the wind is light. The only sail we might add in the future would be a stormsail that hoists over the furler in a special sleeve.

When thinking about sails on a boat, think also about running rigging. Our survey indicated that the running rigging was in acceptable condition but one of the halyards parted almost immediately and we ended up replacing all of the running rigging. There is a reason they say "Boat Bucks" disappear rapidly in a refit. BOAT means Bring On Another Thousand.

Outdoor Water

I read recently that if you want to save money in your cruising kitty that you should buy a really good electric windlass and a really good deck washdown system. The reasoning was that many people end up going to marinas for the night because they're too tired after a day of sailing to deal with the manual windlass and the resulting mess on the deck. The theory is that after a while the cost of marinas would pay for both. I can see the reasoning in this, and both are items that are high on our wish list. As previously mentioned in the hot water section, I would add a cockpit shower to the list as well. Having a shower fixture directly over our hot water heater seems like a much more reasonable arrangement than having it over thirty feet away. This also ties in to the fact that the one big compromise we made in our choice of boat is that we wanted a head at the base of the companionway steps. If it had been there, the hot water would be only a couple feet away.

9 WE BE GYPSIES

It has been nearly five years since we shipped *Kintala* to Lake Carlyle. It was the start of the final push in becoming full time, live-aboard, cruisers. Unbeknownst to us at the time, it was also the start of some of the most difficult years we have known, a monstrously steep climb up a learning curve we did not fully anticipate. That climb lasted through two years of trying to wrestle the Tartan into a safe, reliable, and comfortable sailing vessel we could call home, efforts that went on even after we had launched at Oak Harbor and started living on and sailing her south.

As we work to finish up the cautionary tale of *How* NOT *To Buy A Cruising Boat,* we are cruising the Bahama Islands for a second time. Several really hard sets of circumstances that occurred during our first year out, some that threatened to end our cruising life, are now behind us. Most of those were not directly related to *Kintala's* mechanical condition, though several were based on our learning what it takes to live this life, and live it well. But, no matter how difficult or discouraging the years of working on the boat and first year of being on the water were, one thing cannot be denied...

We made it. We are out here living this life. As I started the first draft of this chapter, *Kintala* was resting easy in the anchorage off Foxtown in the Abaco Islands. With the exception of needing to be back in the States in a few months to try and sell our condo once again, no schedule drives our decisions. There are no bosses to please, no police speed traps set to trip up our day, no commercials demanding that we buy this, no propaganda insisting that what we know to be false is really true, and what we know to be true is really false. Mother Earth and Sister Sea are our closest companions. They determine if our day is to be quiet and easy or a careful watch. Wind and tide help us decide when to move and when to stay put, and very often lead us into places we never expected to be. Often, places we ducked into to sit out some weather turn out to be delightful discoveries, magic places in the world where everything seems to fit just so.

Sometimes, often actually, we end up in a place with a small collection of other cruising boats. Within hours a unique community forms, fellow gypsies making their own way through their own lives, at their own pace, setting their own goals, with their own style. They are as different as they can be, yet share some inner vision that makes for easy companions and life-long friendships. Most share stories similar to ours, straining against the faults in this marine / sailboat business. Yet they too have made it and now belong to this exclusive and very special tribe.

It *is* an exclusive fraternity because the number of people on this planet who have both the desire and the opportunity to live this way is vanishingly small. Though everyone asks what it is like to live on a boat, and many share the dream of "sailing away," very few are serious about making it happen. It is a dream, but in many ways it is a scary dream. It is also a dream difficult to envision even by those who sail regularly. Living and traveling on a boat is as different from weekend pleasure boating or chartering as being a professional athlete is from playing hoops in the local pickup game. The basic skills might be roughly the same, and the courts may be the same size with the basket the same height off the ground as any professional venue. But the reality of living in the professional world has little to do with weekends.

Any community as small as that of full-time cruisers will wield very little political power (visit FL and see) and thus is not a lifestyle any government is particularly interested in supporting or protecting. It is, after all, a community of people who have, at least to some degree, rejected the society they sailed away from. It is a community that looks over the bow to the next destination more than it looks over the stern at what is behind, but "going cruising" and "leaving" are synonymous terms. Doing the former requires that one do that latter. And that is not always an easy thing to do.

Most governments seem uncomfortable with citizens who are independent enough to live like this. It is hard to control a hoard of little boats that make enough electricity for their needs without depending on tightly controlled infrastructures, sometimes make their own fresh water, and often harvest at least some of their own food source from the environment where they live. These same little boats move without roads, going pretty much where and when they please, while leaving little to trace as they go. The ocean itself is a place where marking borders is near impossible. How can a people who live such a life be trusted to support government policies and answer to government mandates?

The devotion of such people to any particular nation is always suspect. Throughout history gypsies have earned a near-universal bad reputation, and the cruising community is no exception. Most are not really scofflaws, not really. It's just that the minutia that governments see as important to holding onto power are unimportant to those who live this close to nature. Check in? Check out? Many of these wanderers see themselves as citizens of the world more than denizens of any particular bit of dirt. Dwellers on the sea that covers the *majority* of the planet, where did land dwellers get the idea that they can "own" a piece of the earth and dictate what goes on there? Governments distrust gypsies for a reason.

After years of visiting boat shows and reading industry media, it does not seem that the marine industry has much more use for cruisers than do governments. The industry doesn't build boats that fit cruiser needs. Day sailing and charter companies fill the corporate coffers, not cruisers out wandering in hulls that are decades old and, usually, modestly equipped. A true cruising boat would be a fully integrated and mobile living system, with solar and wind generating capabilities built in from the start, balanced against efficient onboard systems. Maintenance access would set industry-wide standards, since the sea is a demanding environment and things often break far out of reach of support facilities. As it is, when things break they are often far out of reach of the person who needs to get it fixed, hidden in some deep recess or behind a panel that takes most of a day to remove.

I've never been to a boat show where the boats that are the center of attention sported solar panels or wind generators. Those things are off to the side, hidden among the narrow rows of booths hawking everything from the latest safety harness to a myriad of navigational and communications systems, most of which will not work together on the same boat. And don't trust what the hawkers tell you about their wares, either. We bought a Standard Horizon GX2150 Matrix AIS+ at the Annapolis boat show to add to *Kintala* just before leaving. The young man behind the counter insisted that the radio provided true, *stand-alone*, AIS monitoring, exactly what we were looking to add. But it seemed odd to me that such a system, which had to have stand-alone GPS capability to make the AIS function, would not have some kind of emergency navigation capability as well. So I asked, repeatedly and as pointedly as possible. And each time the young man insisted that yes, it was true *stand-alone*, plug and play, ready to go. So we bought it. And, of course, it was stand-alone except for the GPS input it needed to make the AIS monitoring function.

There are boats very well outfitted for cruising, but they are rarely factory-delivered models. Rather, they are the results of years of "after market" modifications, a patched together, entangled mess of bits and pieces that don't really go together very well. They are mechanical nightmares carrying a dream. *Kintala* is such a boat, as are most of those sailing around her.

And herein lies the most important thing. As much as I hate to admit it, *Kintala* is, in many ways, a patched together mess of a cruising boat. But she carries our dream alive and well. Do I wish the path to this place had been far, far less difficult? Could we have done without the emotional and financial beating administered by an industry apparently set on being as hostile and uncooperative as possible? Of course.

Do I wish Deb had never leaned over the railing of our condo and asked, "What do you think about retiring onto a boat?"

No. It has been the adventure of a lifetime in a life full of adventures. And now I can't imagine never having come this way at all.

10 IT'S ALL GOOD
(Or maybe not)

Dreams are a funny thing. They are at once both powerful and fragile. They have the power to sustain us when we are in a hard place, providing the hope that all humans need to live and the motivation to move in a direction that might be too difficult otherwise. They empower us to accomplish great things for ourselves and for others.

Sometimes dreams are just an escape, our imaginations of possible lives and places. Like picking up a good novel, these dreams give us just the temporary respite we need from a too-long winter or a job which no longer challenges. They are carefully cultivated, evolving as the need for escape changes. They are also highly cherished, eminently private and are never meant to come to pass.

If you're reading this book, I have to assume that one of your dreams is to move onto a cruising yacht and sail somewhere. Just the buying of this book indicates that you've taken a step forward and are seeking to bring your dream to fruition. Your version of this dream may involve selling everything and never looking back, or you might sell *most* everything and store some things in a storage locker "just in case." You might keep that land-based home and rent it temporarily while you try out cruising for a year or two to see if you like it. You might keep a land-based home and commuter cruise half a year, one foot on land, one foot in the boat. Whatever form it takes, know that there is no right way to do it. Every active cruiser out there has modified the form and function of the cruising dream to fit their own particular style, their needs, their financial condition, and their families. The right way is *your* way.

Realizing a dream to go cruising can be one of the most challenging things you've ever undertaken. The sheer logistics of a lifestyle transition such as the one to cruising can be overwhelming. Dealing with all of the associated details will challenge even the most obsessive list maker. Nerves can become frayed, patience thinned, and unless communication is frequent and filled with a boundless sense of humor, relationships can become strained. Regardless of your diligence and preparedness, dreams are always subject to the unpredictable curve balls that life throws at us: medical, financial, familial, and tragedies of all other sorts. We know this up close and personal because of the disaster that was *The Floating Bear*, our kids' boat, detailed on the blog over the months of the summer of 2014. There are, some times, very few good things that one can take away from a broken dream and the temptation is there to lay blame for the failure all on your own shoulders.

Before you think I'm trying to discourage you from buying a cruising yacht and going cruising, I'm not. Undertaking a paradigm shift the likes of cruising hangs you way out over the cliff edge. Some will take the plunge and find happiness, some will test the waters and decide it's just too much risk, or the lifestyle just doesn't fit. But at no point should a cruising dream unrealized be considered a failure. The very dreaming of it, and any attempts to realize it, will offer the dreamer a chance for introspection and a positive change in perspective which is no small accomplishment in our excessively busy society.

We made every mistake in the book while preparing to go cruising, and even made up a few new ones. We suffered setbacks, our "five-year plan" took nearly seven, we are probably on the wrong boat, we never have enough money, things break...and yet I can say without any doubt that no project we've attempted in our 43 years together has yielded the rewards of *The Retirement Project*.

Still want to go cruising? Then dive in, do the best with the information and resources at your disposal and don't look back. You're about to embark on the adventure of a lifetime with a like-minded community to support you every step of the way. And if you happen to see *Kintala* sailing along out there, stop by and we'll lift a cold one to toast your success. See you soon!

It is not the critic who counts, not the one who points out how the strong man stumbled or how the doer of deeds might have done better. The credit belongs to the man who is actually in the arena, whose face is marred with sweat and dust and blood; who strives valiantly; who errs and comes short again and again; who knows the great enthusiasms, the great devotions, and spends himself in a worthy cause; who, if he wins, knows the triumph of high achievement; and who, if he fails, at least fails while daring greatly, so that his place shall never be with those cold and timid souls who know neither victory or defeat.

Theodore Roosevelt

11 COULDN'T HAVE SAID IT BETTER
(Some of the favorite blog posts from
www.theretirementproject.blogspot.com)

After eight years of blog posting, certain individual posts have emerged as the reader favorites. We've reprinted them here for your perusal.

The first is a series of four posts that Tim wrote while dealing with his elderly parents. They required full-time care after some injuries and illnesses, and he traveled back to his hometown to help his sister find a nursing home and to help them make the transition. The pieces are poignant and a tremendous source of information and encouragement for any would-be cruisers who have elderly parents remaining behind.

"Understanding" is a post he did while there, but not specifically related to the nursing home situation.

The post "Dashed Dreams and Pooh-isms" was one of a series of posts about the difficulties our kids and, therefore we, experienced over a boat deal gone bad.

The post "The Voyage" was about my father's passing, a difficult thing for anyone out cruising or preparing to cruise.

"Stuff and Such" was early on, our first thinking about stuff, how much we had accumulated, and how we were going to deal with it.

"The True Cost of Cruising" was done as part of our Cost of Cruising Links page on the blog. Everyone wants to know how much it's going to cost so we started the links side bar. Shortly afterward, Tim wrote that post.

Wednesday, May 14, 2014

Far From Home

Posted by TJ

I am back in the "normal" world for a while; suburbia, cars, traffic jams, sirens, guns, noise, and news. I have put more miles in driving the last 4 days than I had in the last 7 months, and I'm having trouble remembering why I used to enjoy it as much as I did. On the other hand there is ice cream in the fridge, cold milk, (that doesn't cost $12 / gal) and pretty good and consistent Internet access. Not sure the balance comes out in favor of "normal," but it isn't all bad.

Being 1000 miles away from Deb and the ocean? That is pretty much all bad.

Being away is also giving me a chance to take a look at our new life from a little different perspective, an opportunity to think about where we were, where we are, and how it looks like we are doing.

One thing that stands out is that full time living aboard and cruising is a far, far different endeavor than sailing, chartering, or living on a boat as an alternate to having a house or an apartment. It is its own, completely unique, thing. Even more, it is different for every person who is "out there" doing it.

As much as I loved sailing on Carlyle and appreciate the things we did learn about handling and living on a boat there, it really wasn't much preparation for what we are doing now. Having a boat as our one and only home is a far cry from visiting the lake on weekends. Mostly those years allowed us to get a lot of work done on our soon-to-be ocean going house, and make some lifelong friends.

I'm not sure chartering is much like living aboard either. We did take three week-plus training / cruising trips that might be counted as charters. Truth to tell they were not much of a hint as to what living aboard full time is like. Provisioning, watering, finding pump outs, 24 / 7, the 365-days-a-year weather watch, these are our constant companions now. For many of us full time cruising means going "all in." There is no alternative, no plan B, no place to fall back to if it all goes bad. Virtually everything we own floats with *Kintala*. Every weather decision, every day under way, every harbor entered or Current Cut attempted, is an all or nothing deal. Flub it badly and we are homeless...at best.

As valuable as those trips were for us choosing a boat, the fact is both Deb and I are pretty sure the Tartan 42 wasn't the best choice. It is too much the racing boat and not enough the living-on boat. Romping across the Gulf Stream was great. The total time required to go both ways was less than two full days of sailing. (Biscayne Bay to West End + Bimini to Biscayne Bay.)

Living on a Tartan 42 is often a trial, and we do that all the time. For us, a boat just has to be as stable as possible riding to its anchor or a mooring, has to have sufficient storage, and has to have a cockpit comfortable for near full-time occupancy. An island bed would be nice and, contrary to what I had been told, would not be a problem on a passage. Neither of us sleeps in a bed on passage; short handed crews don't often get that far apart.

Once upon a time I claimed a center cockpit boat was a better idea than an aft cockpit, low free board boat because, "I didn't want the ocean that close to my ass." Now I would take an open transom boat without a second thought, so long as the cockpit was big, roomy, and comfortable. It would also make getting on and off the boat from a dink a lot easier. Yet a center cockpit ketch rig would be an excellent basic platform for a live-a-board cruiser. Not because the ocean isn't that close to my ass, but because the sail plan is easy to manage, the aft cabin can be a great place to live, two heads are pretty standard, engine access is likely acceptable, and storage is better.

The cruising community is not much like America. These are people with different motivations, different ideas of what it means to be responsible, with a close and personal relationship with the natural world. Many are from Canada and Europe and are not nearly as impressed with Americans as Americans tend to be with themselves. Most know well their turn will come to need a little help, and so they offer the same with little hesitation.

It isn't that religion and politics are left on the beach, but even among American cruisers no one wears them on their sleeve. There are a few gun nuts, some religious fundamentalists, but none have been offensive or overbearing. Not once have I been told I am going to hell and no one has waved a gun around. Individual political leanings deemed important on land haven't disappeared. But they don't mean as much as they once did. Maybe it's because the ocean will drown Democrats, Republicans, Libertarians, Tea Partiers, Socialists, people who like their universal health care, and even Texans, with equal enthusiasm. Being capable on the water is the measure that matters once any nation and its politics fall below the horizon.

Even for us Americans who have only accomplished a single "ocean crossing" to the Islands and have managed to live there for just a couple of months, the world appears bigger and the center of the map isn't— automatically—the US-of-A. There are whole other societies doing things in a whole other way, with a history completely different from this country. There is a whole planet where people screw things up in new and unique ways, not just American ways. (The Democratic and Republican ways of screwing things up are getting repetitive. We need to come up with some new material.) Being arrogant about "being an American" works inside these borders, where boasting counts more than doing. Outside these borders it makes you look like a wanker.

As much work as living on the water might be, no matter that a different boat might make that life a lot easier, being back for a visit has made it clear that I really don't want to be living anything but a cruising life. Most mornings on *Kintala* I take a cup of coffee out to the cockpit, sit back, and start my day slow and easy. I actually look up to see if it looks like the forecasts are reasonable. The sky and the sea fill my senses. Sometimes we are in the middle of a city, sometimes surrounded by other boats, and sometimes not. Any way I look at it, it is a good way to start a day. Most days end in pretty much the same way except the drink is cold and has a bit more horsepower.

My new world feels far, far, away at the moment, and I long to be home.

Saturday, May 24, 2014

Life is Short...

Posted by TJ

...eat dessert first.

Going cruising revealed that I am not the go-far, off-shore, adventuresome sailor envisioned while plying the fearsome waters of Carlyle Lake. Overnight runs to places not much further than 100 nm miles away are more my speed. One hundred nautical miles is far enough to be out of sight of land for much of a day, or night, and I have had the rare privileged of helming a small boat over the horizon in the deep watches of the dark. It is a magic place out there. What matters and what doesn't is different than on land. On the sea, names mean nothing, neither does history or background, race or religion. All that really matters is that one manage to keep on sailing.

All truly magic places have monsters and demons, things that can challenge and test and frighten those bold enough to venture that way. For sailors there are storms and waves and falling masts. It is part and parcel, these things that can stop the sailing. Magic and monsters go hand in hand.

Where I travel now, magic is hard to come by. Much of my day is spent in a place most sailors dread more than any creature hiding in the deepest ocean, a nursing home. As is my need, I was there today like most days. Lunch was being served in the common room and the room was pretty full. The only person sitting who was not wheelchair-bound was me. At every table were struggles to control utensils and dishes; shaking hands splashed drinks. Bibs were required dress. It was every bit as sad and depressing as it sounds. But as I looked I noticed nearly every person in the room was reaching for the ice cream that came with the meal.

They were eating dessert first.

Just like that, the room was transformed. Instead of tragic, sad old folks struggling to feed themselves, I saw people who have traveled so far over the horizon that names no longer matter, nor history, background, race or religion. All that matters is that they manage to sail just a little bit farther. For some of them, lifting a cup is as physically challenging as getting on deck to reef the main in a sudden blow. For others, walking down a hall is as fraught with danger as climbing a mast in a rolling sea. These may be frail bodies barely holding onto fragile minds, but somewhere at the helm is a will of steel, a courage so deep as to be unfathomable.

Some have gotten so far away that the lines of communication are stretched to the breaking point. They can't tell us of the monsters they face or the demons that haunt their travels. We have no idea how hard it is for them to keep going. Sometimes our courage is no match for theirs, and we fail them by discounting the scale of their journey.

But not all. As I watched some more, I noticed the aids working the room. They knew each patron by name, were unconcerned with spills and stains and shaking hands. Touch was their common language, and smiles, small encouragements and gentle voices spoken loudly. Nursing homes and nursing home workers are often the monsters of our urban tales. But not here, and not in the places I have visited looking for a home for my parents. Sure the monsters lurk, but they are the exception and not the rule. There are Helen and Michael and scores of others who stand their watch without complaint, people who carry part of the burden for those who have traveled so deeply into the night, who see them safely to their final port of call.

Today I had lunch with some of them. And though they will never know it, they served up just enough magic to help me along as well.

Tuesday, June 3, 2014

Tribes and Communities

Posted by TJ

We human beings are tribal animals. Sometimes that is a bad thing, leading to a destructive world view of "us" vs "them." Mostly it is just part of who we are, helping us find a place that fits, setting up the rules of engagement, sorting out who is supposed to do what. We like to imagine we are intelligent creatures, but when it comes to tribal life most of what we do is instinct, bred so deep into our DNA that we don't even notice.

In a simple society, a person belongs to a single tribe. As society gets more complex, any one person becomes a member of overlapping tribes. There are the tribes of work, of home, of church, of the voting booth. There are tribes of pro-this or anti-that, tribes based on skin color, body shape, and chosen method of transportation. Then there are tribes within the tribes: bikers are also sport-bikers or Harley riders, dirt-bikers or those with an Iron Butt. Sometimes these tribes are at cross-purposes. My guess is that a lot of the stress land dwellers know comes from trying to sort out the conflicting demands of the different tribes they call their own.

The cruising community, by its very nature, bucks this trend. The tribe of home is left behind, as is that of work, and of church. This is not to suggest cruisers are a tribe of heathens, but going to the same building with the same people once or twice a week gets a bit difficult when this Sunday finds one in one country, the next in a different country. (Though some of us are, indeed, heathens.) Most human tribes have given up wandering as a life style, the main reason ours is so different.

We do have our stink or stick boaters. But the truth is most live-a-board long term wanderers fly canvas when they can. And many of the tug and trawler crowd flew canvas once upon a time, so the tribal lines are blurred. (Jet skiers need not apply, unless they pull the jet ski behind a boat, not a pick-up truck.) In any case, joining the tribe of cruisers means leaving many other tribes behind.

For weeks now, I have been in this place doing this thing I need to do. I expected it to be a long, sad, somewhat lonely sojourn far from my own tribe. Instead, I found myself part of a completely unexpected, and unsuspected tribe. Tonight, as I was waiting for the elevator, I noticed Grandma and Helen. Grandma speaks okay, but her conversations come from places far away in distance and time. A series of strokes left Helen

113

unable to talk. She makes noises and waves her one good hand. Their wheelchairs were rafted up starboard side to. They were holding hands, clearly communicating; two friends far out to sea, helping each other along. A month ago I would not have noticed what was happening, but I am part of their tribe now. Grandma stops me in the hall to tell me Mom is going to be alright. Helen never fails to notice when I walk by, and I never fail to notice her. Somehow I know her noises and hand waving mean "Hi."

Molly is getting ready to leave the rehab center and move to a nursing home, having mostly overcome the paralysis caused by a stroke. Her boyfriend, Joe, will move with her. They have been together for a long time, and will finish their journey that way as well. I know this because Molly shares a table with Mom for lunch, and we have become friends. Mary has lost parts of both legs to diabetes. She spends much of each day in her chair, wheeling slowly up and down the hall checking things out, stopping to watch, often talking with others in a slow and labored voice. She always stops to talk with me. I always stop to listen. Where a month ago I saw people aimlessly wondering a hallway now, most often, I recognize a person looking for the doorway of a friend.

John once played in the Sugar Bowl. Now he works his legs from a wheelchair, laughing and cracking jokes that, sometimes, only he understands. He is usually in a better mood than is his therapist, which is pretty damned astounding, if you ask me.

All is not sweetness and light. The end of life is the hardest, most harrowing journey of all. Fear is a part of it, as is anger, resentment, and many, many tears. Often the members of this tribe live day-to-day, face-to-face, with a reality the rest of us spend a lifetime trying to ignore. For most this is their one, and last, tribe. But it is a human tribe, perhaps the most human I have ever seen.

I am going to miss these people when I leave. Still, this tribe lives in a hard place of walls and meds and near constant pain. For some of them it is a trial just to get outside, to see the sky without glass in the way, to feel a breeze that isn't coming out of a vent. And in spite of the walls, the seat belts on their chairs, the bars everywhere to keep the standing from falling, the call buttons, and the vigilance of the good folks who oversee this tribe, they sense they are far from safe. This most human of tribes knows a constant danger lurks. They do what they can to face it together.

I will hold the time they accepted me into their tribe as a gift, a chance to learn some things I would never have otherwise learned. But I long to be home, back with the tribe of the open sea. I am not brave enough, or tough enough, to be a true member of this tribe yet.

But they have taught me to be human enough.

Thursday, June 12, 2014

One Last Hero

Posted by TJ

The thing I came here to do is nearly done. In about 48 hours I should be back on board *Kintala* and making plans to push north. It's time to be on the move once again.

While it is long past time for me to be back among my own, I can't really begrudge the last six weeks, even if it did mean being back in a world I don't enjoy. Cars, traffic, noise, crowded buildings, TV, and along with the TV a snoot full of "news." I don't know if anyone else has noticed, but the world is kind of screwed up. The vast majority of the people in the news—world leaders, decision makers, and criminals of all types (some of them the aforementioned world leaders and decision makers)—are pathetically bad excuses for human beings. This is the best we can do? If so, it would seem the human race is bent on making its presence in the cosmos short, unpleasant, and utterly inconsequential. And I have come to accept as a brutal truth an idea I once held as a merely interesting observation: the more power one has, the less human one is. So far as I have seen there are no heroes on the world's stage, just the worst our kind has to offer doing all the harm they can manage.

But that has just been a side-bar observation to doing the thing I needed to do and, like I said, the thing I came here to do is nearly done. Part of winding things up has me joining my parents for their meals at the new home. Seating is arranged to encourage people to be part of the community and my parents share their table with the only other married couple in the place. At the table next to theirs a single woman has sat alone for every meal. That seemed a bit strange to me, so last night I pushed my chair back and met Mary.

Mary is a war widow. Yes, THAT war. As a newlywed she lost her young husband in the Battle of the Bulge. She never remarried. You can see why in the echo of the love that still shines in her eyes these seven decades after her loss. Her brother was killed in that war as well, though she didn't tell me exactly where or how.

Alone, Mary raised a daughter who never knew her father. She told me her story without a hint of self-pity or a single word of complaint. In fact, she smiled a lot, and laughed, and explained that she normally sat alone because many of the others are uncomfortable around her. Having spent some time with her, my guess is they are just worn down by her exuberance. I am 30+ years her junior and can usually hold my own

115

when it comes to slinging words, but I was hard pressed to volley some of her serves. Her court is no place for the timid or the shy. And while I believe I held up the honor of telling sailor's tales well, I had no match for her life's story or the style with which she has lived it. Somehow, in a life marred with a hurt too deep for me to imagine, she found joy enough to share.

I'm going home soon, but I got the chance to meet one last hero before I do.

Tuesday, May 20, 2014

Understanding

Posted by TJ

It has been a bit surprising, the reactions people have when they find out they are talking with someone who lives full time on a sailboat. About half exclaim that they could never do such a thing, and then go on about how cool it must be. The other half go on about how cool it must be, and then get a bit whimsical about doing it themselves. If the situation allows, it will take a while to get away as each will want to hear all about storms and pirates on the one hand, beaches and resorts on the other.

Which usually leads to them being a tiny bit disappointed. Cruisers are pretty good at avoiding storms and pirates, don't have as much time for beaches as non-cruisers imagine, and don't often care much about visiting resorts. Somehow people who live in houses with a thousand square feet of living space imagine that a 42-foot sailboat is large, that life on the ocean is easy, filled with cold drinks, fantastic food, and beautiful people. All-day excursions to go shopping, humping water on and trash off, munching soggy crackers to fend off motion sickness on a bumpy night passage, and all the other joys of this life that cruisers know so well, come as a huge surprise to those who live in big boxes with yards. Yet almost all still think it is cool when the conversation ends.

Another near-universal question is what our plans are, where are we going next? Trying to give an honest answer goes something like this:

"Well, for the rest of the summer it looks like South Carolina will be home base for some boat work. Come fall, Biscayne Bay until the New Year, then probably over to the Islands again. The Abacos are fantastic, but friends have talked up the Exumas and it sounds like they shouldn't be missed. The goal come next Spring will be heading to the Northern Chesapeake to park the boat for a while; overland to St. Louis to try and sell the condo in June. By the end of 2015 Kintala could be back in southern FL looking forward to a third winter in the Islands. Spring 2016 she might be heading farther south, instead of north, to hide from hurricanes. Maybe we will make Central America for the summer of 2016; live in another country for a while. After that, who knows?"

To a cruiser's ear this is a perfectly normal sounding response. But to those living the American Dream it sounds like the ravings of the demented. "Looks like," "should," "could," South Carolina, Biscayne Bay, Exumas, Abaco, Chesapeake, 2015, 2016, Central America...The stark difference between the old life on land and the new one on the water is plain as their eyes glaze over and the wheels turn trying to figure out where some of those places are. "Planning" years into the future to be in locations we have never seen, while not really knowing where we will be in a week or a month?

This is a very odd way to live, and I have about given up on the idea of getting those who haven't done it to understand. Not a big surprise. After 7 years of preparing, shedding nearly everything we knew, and now having almost a year and 2000 nm in our log, I am just beginning to understand it myself.

This is also a very tenuous way to live. The ocean environment is what it is with complete disregard to anything else. We see it as beautiful, challenging, compelling; as well as uncaring, uncomfortable, and quite easily deadly. But that is only land-living unmasked. For example, I have two grandkids now living on a sailboat. Many have commented on how dangerous that is. Really? In a society of cars, guns, and gangs just how dangerous is the ocean by comparison? And those cars, guns, and gangs are nearly as hazardous to adults as they are to children. Living on the ocean means admitting life is fleeting and capricious instead of living on land and pretending life is permanent and predictable.

For many of us, getting here means dumping most of the material things that make up American life. Houses, cars, furniture, yards, gardens, swimming pools, monster grills that fill the patio, the patio itself...none of that stuff fits on the common cruising boat. We cut the ties to stuff, and many of us are surprised to discover the idealism of our youth was more righteous than we thought. We should have stuck with it from the very beginning. Sadly, we missed the chance to teach this old / new idea to our kids. They are already buried under mountains of student loans and struggling to survive the class warfare of corporate America. But we have grandkids...

From the back yards of suburbia and through the eye of the TV tube, America is a big place and the world is kind of small. From the deck of a sailboat and through the eyes that nature gave us, the world is a big place and America is kind of small. And I mean "small" in more ways than just geography. Once upon a time a collection of Americans brought out the best in each. Now, collectively, we are mean spirited and narrow minded. Dreams of greatness have been replaced by delusions of grandeur. Once we had hope. Now we just hope for the best.

Literally yards off shore that starts to fade. People keep an eye out for trouble, step in and help when they can. There are lots of smiles, waves, and greetings. Complete strangers-soon-to-be-friends will stop by in a dink to ask about the boat or comment on the home port listed on the stern. Stories of places far away will be shared, and the idea of visiting them will be encouraged. Before we left, a lot of people said we shouldn't go, that we weren't ready. Once we did go, the cruiser community encouraged us to keep going. This is a life of bold people doing a different thing.

There is a sometimes cruiser custom that I love. As the sun touches the horizon in the west, conch horns sound to herald the close of another day...*"We are with the tribe, riding safe to anchor or mooring, thankful for the challenges of the day, and content with the peace that comes with the night."*

Hard to explain to those who haven't been here.

Friday, July 11, 2014

Dashed Dreams and Pooh-isms

Posted by Deb

It starts as a thought. Sometimes it's as nebulous as a fleeting image amid the shifting colors and shapes that frequent our closed eyes, those ones in that few moments between the sigh of stretching out in bed after a long day and the blessed descent into deep sleep. Sometimes it's a nagging poke in our busy, workaday consciousness demanding attention when we have little to give, plaguing us like a fly at which we swat, irritated.

The Thought falls on fertile ground. The thought lurks in the darkness of the fertile soil, tenuous little shoots breaking through the hard shell of the seed to take root, small ones at first that will grow with water and sunshine.

The Thought becomes an idea. The Idea can't be ignored. It's a force to be reckoned with, pushing aside meetings, appointments, to-do lists, and schedules. You begin to hear musings like, "What if?" and "Maybe we could..." and "I'll look on yachtworld.com, you know, just to see what's out there..."

The Idea becomes a dream. The Dream is all-encompassing. It involves your desire to live with less: less of a carbon footprint, less money, less "stuff" as an encumbrance, less stress. It might involve looking to travel. It might involve looking to escape. It might mean looking for a place to live with a view. You look at big boats you can't possibly ever hope to afford. You look at boats with all the comforts of home. You look at staunch blue water sailboats because you aspire to be Joshua Slocum. You pour over maps and glossy magazines with pictures of white, sandy beaches and aquamarine waters. Your umbrella drink is already in your hand as you swing in the hammock in the shade of a coconut palm.

The Dream becomes a plan. The Plan is usually the oft-intoned 5-year plan. Five years to look for and buy a boat, to take sailing classes, to purge yourselves of "stuff", finish out your employment, move aboard, and cast off the dock lines. Ambitious? Yes. Doable? Yes.

In the same way as the seedling, this process is fragile and fraught with opportunities to fail. The process requires a mind open to new possibilities, to adventure, to change. It requires constant care. It requires thoughtful and careful choices, and it requires a tremendous amount of luck. Remove any of these and the beauty of a dream can fall by the

120

wayside like so much refuse.

Our kids came dangerously close to this cliff yesterday. We hauled *The Floating Bear* out at a local marina in Ft. Lauderdale where they had made arrangements with a local mechanic to fix some of the more pressing issues so they could get on their way to their lives in Coconut Grove. The news was bad. In fact, the news was about as bad as it gets. The boat needs much more work than they anticipated, much more work than they have the financial resources to pay for, and even the mechanic who would be the beneficiary of the large check advised that our money would be better spent on another boat rather than the current money pit that is *The Floating* Bear. The Dream spiraled downward ever faster as the afternoon turned into evening and conversations became less hopeful.

Right around this time, as Tim and I walked back from the marina lounge, we happened to stop to chat with our friend Gilles, a full-time resident at the marina. Not being financially or emotionally involved in the drama of the *Bear*, he was able to offer some rather sage advice. He asked what their goal was.

Epiphany. We had lost site of the goal. The kids' goal was to find a sustainable, affordable way of living that would allow them to pursue their dream of writing and painting. While they love the idea of a sailboat and its way of fitting into nature in such a way as to compliment it rather than destroy it, they don't need a sailboat right now. They need a place to live. *The Floating Bear* didn't need to be *The Sailing Bear*. *Very* nearly all of the major repairs were related to *The Bear's* ability to ply the waters elegantly with canvas. Desirable? Yes. Necessary to reach the goal? No.

Discussions picked up this morning. Ideas were flung around, modified, tested, held up to the light, and some discarded. A hint of hope sifted through the conversation. The Dream began to be restored and a new Plan evolved. Tomorrow the *Bear* will begin the transformation from sailing boat to floating home and, as it is the home of an artist, a writer, and two small Pooh fans, it will undoubtedly be as creative as the original *Floating Bear*. The *Bear's* days of sailing are over, but like its namesake, I think *The Bear* will carry her family safely through the floods that have been threatening, and when passersby exclaim that something (the mast) is missing from *The Bear*, they will have Pooh's words handy for retort: "I ought to say," explained Pooh as they walked down to the shore of the island, "that it isn't just an ordinary sort of boat."

Wednesday, November 24, 2010

The Voyage

Posted by Deb

I've been thinking a lot about the voyage these days. I read a lot about cruisers who rush here and rush there and bypass things worth seeing so they can get somewhere else on schedule, something that seems to me to be a trip to a destination, not a voyage.

My ruminations on the voyage have taken a detour these days, though, as I've been sitting with my dad in the cardiac ICU in Pittsburgh, PA where I was born. Time is suspended when you sit there. You're not allowed to have your cell phone, which happens to also be my watch, it's generally dark in the room, and there's a lot of white noise that blurs the edges a little, leaving you only vaguely aware that there's life outside the room.

My dad's voyage is nearing its end. His life has been full, vital, meaningful, worthy. He has taught me the value of hard work, the love of nature, the patience of fishing, and the respect of all peoples regardless of color or nationality. He gave me the opportunity to live in a foreign country for a good part of my formative years, helping me to value my freedom in a way not possible without that experience, to see how much we take for granted in this land where we sometimes treat the cost of freedom with casual indifference. His background in engineering is responsible for my intense curiosity. He gave me the gift of all the tools I needed to explore, and none of the reprimand if I happened only to succeed in dismantling something but fell short of its repair. I see him shudder as he labors to take a breath and I wish that just this once the doctors could repair *him*.

As a cruiser who hasn't left the land yet, there's a tendency to be waiting for the voyage to begin. Everything is geared toward "When we make the break from land...", but sitting here and looking back on my dad's life, I'm reminded that every minute of every day we voyage, whether we wring the most out of it or waste it, or just plain miss it. So stop, take a deep breath, take a look around you and smile at someone. Look at the sunset, feel the rain on your face, smell the coffee wafting out of the Starbucks, listen to the laughter of the neighbor kids, smell the ocean. You may only have this minute. Today. Or you might be really, really blessed and have 85 years to soak it all in.

Stuff-and-Such

Posted by Deb

When I was growing up, my grandmother (who was quite a character) used to talk about "Stuff-and-Such," meaning all the mounds of accumulated things that end up surrounding us. She was, after all, an expert in the matter. All the reading about living aboard a sailboat and the simplified life aboard caused a great amount of philosophical rumination on the subject recently, which culminated in a long weekend of dealing with said "Stuff-and-Such." I faced the garage storage compartment with a great deal of courage, large trash bags, empty Goodwill boxes, and a space designated on the floor with each child's name. Things I learned in the process:

- If your garage burned down and you never had a chance to look in these boxes you'd never miss what was inside of them. The matches mocked me every time I passed them throughout the day.

- Personal shredders should have been invented a long time ago.

- If your child asks you if she can store something at your house, tell her that if it's not important enough for her to have in her house, it's not important enough for you to have in your garage.

- Spiders already have enough homes to live in without you providing a box of Christmas ornaments that you never intend to use.

- I could buy a lot of stuff for a boat with the money I would have saved not renting storage centers over the years.

- If I haven't opened a box in 3 moves I should throw it away immediately.

- Never, ever should I let things or the acquiring of them become more important than people.

Don't get me wrong. Not all "things" collected are bad. Objects have a tremendous power to connect us to memories of good times past and to people we love. I tore open one box of things I'd saved for the kids' kids only to find mixed in with the stuffed animals an old, ratty red hooded sweatshirt that belonged to my mother. She wore it in a picture that I have of her raking leaves on a beautiful fall day. It was one of the last healthy, happy days of her life before she had her stroke. I cried for half an hour. The key is in determining what things are worth saving and what things are not, and the reality of it is that, in the end, we can take nothing with us at all. So as I begin the long, long (did I say long?) process of reduction, I'm trying on the liveaboard life a little at a time, anticipating the tremendously liberating feeling of living life as it should be—hard work with your hands, a close tie to nature, and time with loved ones. It just doesn't get much better than that.

Thursday, August 29, 2013

The True Cost of Cruising

Posted by TJ

Two Daughters and five grandkids...today was the day we said the rest of the hard good-byes. I was doing okay right through the day, playing, reading books, explaining to the two oldest girls why we were staying at a marina they had never visited and then explaining about travel lifts and trucks. But at the end of the day, just when it looked like I might hold it together the youngest, with no clue what he was about to do to my heart, crawled to my feet, held his arms up to be lifted, then tucked his face into my shoulder....

There is no explanation for the wanderer's soul. There is no cure for wanderlust. I have been unhappy being in one place since (so I am told anyway) my first day of first grade. Less than an hour of being penned in one room and I had had enough. The twelve years that followed, all in the same school district, were pure misery. It showed in my grades, in my list of detentions, in the fights and the brushes with police. I was that kid none of the other kids were allowed to hang out with. Quite literally, they let me out after my Senior year because no one wanted to see me there again.

The two years of technical school were a slight improvement; partly because I was the kid right out of high school in a class mostly made up of people recently out of the jungles of 'Nam. They were a tough lot, several more than a little crazy, many of whom took a liking to the combative kid who (I now suspect) reminded them of themselves before someone started shooting at them. It also helped that only half our day was spent in a classroom; the other half we spent out in the shop. Still penned in, but better than a desk. To this day, no one knows how often I dreamed of just walking away from that place and how close I came to doing it...the future I hoped to share with Deb being the only thing that kept me going back.

They let us "graduate" a few weeks early to fill jobs rebuilding B-52s. Deb and I headed west and never looked back. We spent 4 years in one place, 14 in another, 2 in a third, then landed in St. Louis. But we wandered constantly: me as a pilot, both of us as bikers. And no place ever felt like a "home," just a town with a job.

Now, finally, we are on the verge of heading off again; this time for a wanderer's dream come true. No place is home, but anywhere can be our front yard. The challenge of new skills to learn, the lure of new places to

125

see, experiencing life in a way unsuspected just six years ago, and no one can tell us we have to "stay here and do this." But the dream has a price just shy of being too high—a price no one but a wanderer would even think about paying.

We like to say that there is no choice, that the wanderer wouldn't be the person he or she is if they could stop. Perhaps that is true. We are going, after all. But I like to think that the price will be a fair one. That in the end the people we love who don't wander with us love us anyway; that they share our adventures and find a larger view of the world. That, in the end, the stories of our lives will be full, even if the main characters in our hearts are not written into every page.

For that is the true cost of cruising.

RESOURCES

Weather

1. www.noaa.gov

2. www.nhc.noaa.gov (Hurricane Center)

3. NOAA NOW Android App

4. Pocket Grib Android / iOS App

5. www.weatherbug.com

6. www.wunderground.com

7. Marine Weather by Accuweather Android / iOS App

8. HF Weather Fax app for iOS and Android to record short wave receiver weather faxes

9. Windguru Android App

10. PredictWind iOS App

Navigation

1. Garmin BlueChart Mobile for iOS

2. Navionics App for Android / iOS

3. ActiveCaptain.com

4. Smart Chart AIS for Android

5. Open CPN

Maintenance

1. www.pbase.com/mainecruising

2. *The Complete Illustrated Sailboat Maintenance Manual* by Don Casey

3. *How Boat Things Work* by Charlie Wing

4. *Marine Diesel Engines* by Nigel Calder

5. *Sailmaker's Apprentice* by Emiliano Marino

6. *Boater's Pocket Reference* by Thomas McEwen

ABOUT THE AUTHORS

Deb and Tim (TJ) Akey were never on a sailboat until their first sailing class in 2007. The dream to retire early onto a sailboat was Deb's, but Tim was immediately supportive. They bought their starter sailboat, a Compac 27, in 2008 and learned to live aboard, sail, and maintain her. In 2011 they purchased a Tartan 42 named *Kintala*, and began prepping her for full-time cruising. They were hoping to cast off the dock lines early in 2015 but a department restructuring in Tim's company left him unexpectedly unemployed in 2013. Faced with the decision to get other jobs or leave early, they decided that they would never have "enough" money, and the boat would never be "ready," so they decided to leave. They departed their home marina, Boulder Marina in Boulder, IL, on Tim's 58th birthday in July of 2013, and after a 10-week boat yard tour launched *Kintala* into the Chesapeake at Oak Harbor Marina in Pasadena, MD on October 19, 2013. During the first year of cruising they motored the ICW, toured anchorages and mooring fields in Florida, took a multiple-month trip to the Bahamas, then found themselves pinned to a dock due to family travails. Their year anniversary was spent looking forward to many more months of white, sandy beaches and aquamarine waters in the Islands for their second year of cruising. To follow along on their continuing journey, you can visit their blog:

www.theretirementproject.blogspot.com

Made in the USA
San Bernardino, CA
26 November 2018